THE
POC[
IDIOT'S
GUIDE™ TO

ALPHA BOOKS

Published by the Penguin Group

Penguin Group (USA) Inc., 375 Hudson Street, New York, New York 10014, USA

Penguin Group (Canada), 90 Eglinton Avenue East, Suite 700, Toronto, Ontario M4P 2Y3, Canada (a division of Pearson Penguin Canada Inc.)

Penguin Books Ltd., 80 Strand, London WC2R 0RL, England

Penguin Ireland, 25 St. Stephen's Green, Dublin 2, Ireland (a division of Penguin Books Ltd.)

Penguin Group (Australia), 250 Camberwell Road, Camberwell, Victoria 3124, Australia (a division of Pearson Australia Group Pty. Ltd.)

Penguin Books India Pvt. Ltd., 11 Community Centre, Panchsheel Park, New Delhi—110 017, India

Penguin Group (NZ), 67 Apollo Drive, Rosedale, North Shore, Auckland 1311, New Zealand (a division of Pearson New Zealand Ltd.)

Penguin Books (South Africa) (Pty.) Ltd., 24 Sturdee Avenue, Rosebank, Johannesburg 2196, South Africa

Penguin Books Ltd., Registered Offices: 80 Strand, London WC2R 0RL, England

Copyright © 2005 by Jennifer Basye Sander and Peter Sander

THE POCKET IDIOT'S GUIDE TO and Design are trademarks of Penguin Group (USA) Inc.

International Standard Book Number: 978-1-59257-435-3
Library of Congress Catalog Card Number: 2005930987

10 09 08   8 7 6 5

Interpretation of the printing code: The rightmost number of the first series of numbers is the year of the book's printing; the rightmost number of the second series of numbers is the number of the book's printing. For example, a printing code of 05-1 shows that the first printing occurred in 2005.

Printed in the United States of America

Note: This publication contains the opinions and ideas of its authors. It is intended to provide helpful and informative material on the subject matter covered. It is sold with the understanding that the authors and publisher are not engaged in rendering professional services in the book. If the reader requires personal assistance or advice, a competent professional should be consulted.

The authors and publisher specifically disclaim any responsibility for any liability, loss, or risk, personal or otherwise, which is incurred as a consequence, directly or indirectly, of the use and application of any of the contents of this book.

Most Alpha books are available at special quantity discounts for bulk purchases for sales promotions, premiums, fund-raising, or educational use. Special books, or book excerpts, can also be created to fit specific needs.

For details, write: Special Markets, Alpha Books, 375 Hudson Street, New York, NY 10014.

Contents

Introduction

So there you were, browsing the shelves at your local bookstore, when suddenly you spied the very sort of book you'd been looking for—a book all about living on a budget. Never mind the jammed shelves of books on all manner of topics—from sailing to scandal (with a wide variety of chicken soups)—what you need is a book to help you get a handle on your money. A handle on your life.

Does this mean you must be broke? Heck, no! There are a zillion reasons to want to live on a budget, most of them good. Given the choice between living prudently (and sleeping soundly at night) and squandering all your resources in an endless cycle of consumption and debt, which sounds like the better idea?

Does this mean you'll have to give up all the good things in life and live in strict adherence to a written budget? Endless evenings of examining columns of figures and making small notations with a red pencil? Not at all.

As you'll learn in the coming pages, there are folks who have lived successfully on a budget for many years without ever having written anything down. There are folks with modest incomes who, because they've lived by a sensible budget, are able to live a much richer life than you'd imagine. There are also folks who choose to live on a modest budget and invest the rest of their income to opt out of the race early and retire long before their friends and neighbors could afford to. Why struggle to "keep up with the Joneses" when you can smile and wave bye-bye to them as you drive away to your new life of leisure?

You'll soon see that, once you have a basic grasp of the principles behind living on a budget, practicing it will become second-nature, and you probably won't notice that much of a difference in your lifestyle, other than a sense of financial peace of mind.

Will we be lecturing you about excess consumption and an American society gone mad with the foolish desire to accumulate stuff? Oh, a little bit, perhaps.

Will we be asking you to become monklike in your lifestyle, eschewing all but the basics? No. It just isn't necessary. We'll ask you instead to embrace wisdom and discipline, not austerity.

Here's what this book will ask you to do: Take a clear-eyed look at the way you live your life and the way you want your life to be. And then we'll help you create a day-to-day financial lifestyle that helps you make the shift from where you are to where you *want* to be. Sound simple? It is.

How to Use This Book

This book walks you through the basics of budgeting step by step. Nothing too fancy, nothing that requires a slide rule (do they still make those things?). We'll start off with a close look at what's going on in your life now and how to make changes. Then we will fill your mind (and, we hope, refill your wallet) with many ways to shave costs on everyday expenses and help you understand how to lay a solid foundation for your financial future.

But Wait, There's More!

Sprinkled within these pages, you will find a few types of information:

Moneywise Meanings

Definitions of terms, words, and phrases that help you grasp the concepts discussed here.

Budget Bombs

Cautionary tales about sure-fire ways to blow your money.

123 By the Numbers

Stories and advice from folks who've been budgeting successfully for years and years.

Savvy Saver

Tips and tricks on saving money across the board.

Acknowledgments

We'd like to thank our parents—Jerry Sander and Betty Gwyn, and George and Mary Alice Basye—for helping us understand from an early age that money was not something to be tossed around carelessly. We hope we can pass that same message along to our two boys, Julian and Jonathan.

Special thanks to C. Herbert Feltner and David Brown for ensuring the technical accuracy of this book.

Trademarks

All terms mentioned in this book that are known to be or are suspected of being trademarks or service marks have been appropriately capitalized. Alpha Books and Penguin Group (USA) Inc. cannot attest to the accuracy of this information. Use of a term in this book should not be regarded as affecting the validity of any trademark or service mark.

Why You *Might* Need This Book

In This Chapter

- Why budgets are a good idea
- What married couples really fight about
- How budgeting will earn you treats
- Why little expenses mean big headaches

"Living on a budget": The very phrase conjures up grim visions of taking the bus to work, suffering through endless meals of beans and rice, and carefully reusing your vacuum cleaner bags.

But is this what living on a budget is really all about? We, your erstwhile authors, don't believe so (or else we wouldn't be living on one!). We believe that living on a budget is about wisdom and discipline, not about deprivation.

Living on a budget simply means making a conscious decision to keep a close eye on your income and expenses and making sure you don't spend too much of one on the other! That, in a nutshell, is what budgeting is all about. It's not about buying shoddy goods, and it's not about leading a dull life of austerity. It's about mastering your money and making the most of every dollar you have.

Budgeting works. Regardless of the size of your income, budgeting works. Join us now to learn more about living happily on a budget.

Why Budget?

So who needs to live on a *budget?* Everyone who wants to feel in control of his or her finances, anyone who wants to take pride in watching his or her money grow from month to month, instead of watching the money dissolve, and folks who are trying to do the following:

- Conquer the onslaught of monthly bills.
- Lower living expenses with the goal of increasing savings.
- Achieve a dream of early retirement.
- Opt out of the shop-and-spend cycle.
- Save for a major purchase like a car or a house.
- Achieve other financial goals.

Moneywise Meanings _____

Budget—A simple financial plan that helps you track your expenses and income to achieve financial goals.

The bottom line is that living on a budget is for anyone interested in his or her bottom line!

123 By the Numbers _____

"What I want more than anything is to wake up in nine years and have the ultimate luxury—the freedom to spend my time doing anything I want to do," reads a recent letter to the editor of a popular financial magazine. The letter-writer describes himself as earning a six-figure income, but living as though he makes $25,000 a year. He is 41 now, and by carefully living on a budget, he plans to retire at the ripe old age of 50.

Ever Run Out of Money Before You Run Out of Month?

It's a classic scenario, one that has happened to almost every adult at one time or another: suddenly, you discover that the checking account balance is at zero, your bills are all due, and your next paycheck isn't coming for another week or so. It is *not* a pleasant feeling, and not at all conducive to a restful night's sleep. Many of us face this same situation every month, like clockwork. What to do? *Budget!*

By drawing up a simple budget plan, vowing to stick with it, and then following through, even folks who face this dire situation every month will be sleeping through the night in no time.

By vowing to live on a budget, you can soon get a handle on all your bills—even past-due bills—and pay them off in a timely manner. Once you embrace the idea of living on a budget, you can also work to overcome the spending habits that got you into trouble in the first place.

So go ahead, open those bills! Ahhh, doesn't that sound like a much more appealing scenario? Imagine your pride when you open each month's bills without apprehension, knowing that you can pay them with ease.

Men, Women, and Money

The Macy's bill arrives in the mail … and someone goes ballistic at the sight of the balance. Perhaps a husband is horrified by his wife's shopaholic habits. Could just as easily be a wife annoyed by her husband's profligate ways, though. Whoever is out there doing the spending, there's bound to be a fight when the bill finally arrives.

What do most American couples fight about? Money. From the tippy-top of the economic strata and on down through the rest of the classes, almost every married couple fights about money.

Seven out of Ten

Here is a quick snapshot from a recent *USA Today* article. They discovered that seven out of ten couples disagree about financial issues. The most common conflicts occur over the following issues:

- The use of credit (17 percent)
- Shopping and spending habits (16 percent)
- Sticking to a budget (13 percent)
- Not writing down checks, and bouncing checks (8 percent)
- Paying bills (7 percent)
- Saving and investing (6 percent)

How can couples escape all this conflict? *Budget!* In Chapter 3 we also discuss how to agree with your mate about setting family goals and sticking to a budget. Budgets don't work unless everyone involved pulls together.

Couples fight about money for all kinds of reasons. Sometimes it's about emotions, sometimes about power and control, sometimes about love—and sometimes those fights about money end in divorce.

Budget Therapy

However, couples can use money to strengthen their relationship, to grow even closer. By working together to create a budget that meets their needs, by agreeing to live by the basic budgeting principles, and by focusing on the mutual financial benefit they are working toward, couples can use living on a budget to enhance their relationship. You will soon find that what's good for your relationship is good for your *net worth*, too!

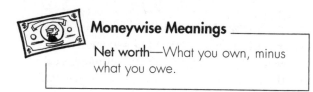

Moneywise Meanings

Net worth—What you own, minus what you owe.

Treat Yourself

Seems like all you do is wake up, eat, work, eat, work, eat, watch a little television, and sleep. Your life is just an endless cycle of drudgery, and all your money goes just to support your dull life the way it is. Will you never get to jog on the beach in Hawaii? Will you never feel the wind in your face as you drive along the coast in a convertible? Sigh. You just plain can't afford those kinds of treats. Other people can, but you feel destined to watch from the sidelines. Hmmm … what's the answer here? Surprise—*budget!*

Careful budgeting can help you achieve extraordinary financial goals. Vacations, second homes, a really cool car—whatever you set out to save for can be accomplished by carefully sticking to a budget and watching your special savings grow.

Cheap Thrills

Careful budgeting can also help you rediscover that some of life's greatest rewards come free. You might well find that your idea of a treat turns out to be a morning walk in the woods near your home, an afternoon at the public library, or an evening at home in front of a roaring fire with friends and a battered Monopoly set. While living on a budget and watching your money grow, you might realize that the kinds of treats and indulgences that truly make you happy can't be found in a department store, at a mall, or in the pages of a catalog.

After you wean yourself from some of the spending habits you once had, not only will your bills be paid off, but you also won't ever run them up again with those kinds of expensive purchases.

Budget Bombs

Most married couples disagree about money at some point in their relationship. Unless both parties agree to follow the same budget, the effort is doomed to fail. The most common cause of financial disagreement? Credit-card spending.

Not So Cheap Thrills

Not all of life's great rewards do come free, though. Once you've worked your way through the budgeting philosophy in this book we will reward you with information about how to score some thrills for less. We've included a whole section on how to save money on massages, manicures, designer clothes, and other goodies. Just a little something extra for you to anticipate as you get your spending and saving under control!

Budgeting and saving sound like something only middle-class folks have to do. The really rich folks just spend whatever they want, right? Wrong. According to an item in *Business Week* magazine, the rich squirrel money away much more than other income levels do. So next time you want to be mistaken for a wealthy person, drive straight to the bank and make a deposit. And stay away from that ATM machine while you're there!

The Fritterer

Perhaps you don't have a shopping-mall addiction or a tendency to live well beyond your means. Regardless of your careful shopping habits, however, you still find that at the end of the month the money seems to have disappeared. Where on Earth did it go? Perhaps you simply frittered it away a dollar or two at a time.

What do we mean by "frittering"? You know: the Starbucks Syndrome. Our friend David Bach, author of *The Automatic Millionaire*, calls this the "Latte Factor." Money can all too easily be frittered away every time you rush out the door late to work and pull into the café drive-through lane for a cappuccino and a low-fat muffin. Money can be frittered away if you buy a new magazine every day to keep you company at lunch. And then there's the nightly visit to a sports bar for a beer and a plate of Buffalo chicken wings. One dollar here, two dollars there—it can all add up to the difference between ending the month with extra money and ending the month with zip.

Frittering is sometimes hard to spot. Later in the book, we cover the importance of writing down *all* your expenditures to get a real idea of where the money is going. This way, you can quickly uncover frittering.

A Clear-Eyed View of the Present

So let's get down to business here. Have you recognized yourself in any of the descriptions we've offered so far? Are you in over your head because of excess shopping? Do you and your mate tangle regularly over financial matters? Are you just "getting by" on your current salary? Or are you just looking for a more reasonable way to live? Whatever your reasons for deciding to live on a budget, you've come to the right book.

As we've already hinted, we don't think that living on a budget means scrimping and saving and buying only the very cheapest stuff. We believe that living on a budget is a wise approach to handling your money in today's economy, and we plan to show you exactly how you can use a budget to create the life you want.

But first, you have to look closely at the life you have now. In the next few chapters, we walk you through a careful assessment of your present financial situation. Why does that matter? Because you can never design a workable budget without first assessing your life and your relationship to money. If you're spending thousands of dollars a month more than you earn, then designing a budget that reduces your expenses to less than $500 a month is doomed to fail. Realistic, steady goals and objectives are needed for a budget to succeed. Remember what we all know about weight loss—crash diets don't work. And neither does a crash money diet.

Learning more about how you use money now is such an important piece of the puzzle that we don't actually help you design your first budget until Chapter 5. (No skipping ahead!) Learn all you can about your family spending habits and the way you use money now. All the thinking and soul-searching will pay off in the long run. You will end up with a renewed sense of what's possible to achieve on your income—the very thing that seems so impossible now!

A Misty-Eyed View of the Future

Before we go on to the next chapter, let's spend some time thinking about just what living on a budget can do for you. The best way to convince yourself to buckle down and change your money habits is to paint a vivid picture in your mind of just where it's going to lead.

If, starting now, you make the decision to begin to live on a reasonable budget, then this is what your life can be like:

- You will sleep easily at night and never be plagued by anxiety and stress over how you're going to pay that looming bill.

- You will take pride in your skill at handling your family finances and not be ashamed or afraid that you might someday be revealed as financially incompetent.

- Never again will you watch nervously as the sales clerk runs your credit card through the machine, fearing the possibility of rejection.

- By carefully building up reserves and emergency funds, you will be able to deal with financial emergencies and not find yourself wrecked by the first unexpected bill that comes up.

- By working with your mate to design a budget you can both live with, you will no longer live in a household where money is an issue.

- Through careful planning, you *will* be able to give yourself life's little treats, as well as some of life's big ones. You really will be able to afford that (fill in the blank with your deepest desire) you've always wanted.

- By careful budgeting, saving, and investing, you can look forward to a peaceful retirement without worrying how to pay for it.

Sounds darn good, doesn't it? So what are we waiting for—let's get in there and start to work on a budget!

The Least You Need to Know

- Living on a budget doesn't mean depriving yourself of life's pleasures.
- Everyone, regardless of income, can benefit by adopting the basic principles of budgeting—living within your means and having something left over at the end of the month.
- Living on a budget helps you avoid the "run out of money before you run out of month" syndrome.
- Most couples fight about money, so agreeing to live with a reasonable budget can lessen that relationship tension and stress.
- Sometimes the culprit is not spending too much money on big purchases, but spending too much money on little purchases.

Chapter 2

But I'm Not an Accountant

In This Chapter

- The budget philosophy explained
- Why watching TV makes you spend
- Discovering your spending pitfalls
- Budgets aren't hard, aren't boring, and don't even need to be in writing

Budgeting sounds great so far, doesn't it? It sounds like a way to ease the financial stress in your life, a way to slowly get closer to your big financial goals, a way to declare to the world that you are fully in charge and a person to be reckoned with. Well, budgeting will help with the first two, anyway!

Don't Get Your Pencil Out Yet

Before we get down to the serious business of helping you design a budget that is just right for you and your needs, we're going to give you a bit of background behind the philosophy of budgeting.

Once our lecture is through, we'll again ask you to turn the searchlight on yourself, your money habits, and your family's money habits, too, if you've got more than one hand going into your wallet. No matter how elaborate a budget plan you design for yourself, it's destined to fail if you design it without regard to the way you and your family think about money.

> **Budget Bombs**
>
> All your budgeting intentions and resolutions won't help one iota unless you make a plan and stick with it! A plan isn't a plan unless you plan to do it.

"Living on a Budget" Philosophy

In Chapter 1, we scoffed at the notion that living on a budget means eating rice and beans while shivering at the table in a room with the heat turned down low. Sounds like a scene from a Dickens novel! Not the sort of lifestyle you were hoping this book would lead you to.

Far from it. We truly do believe that budgets lead to just the opposite of a meager lifestyle. Pull up a chair and we'll tell you why.

Money Conscious

To begin living on a budget, you must first develop *awareness*. You must develop not only an awareness of your current financial situation, income, expenses, and habits, but also a keener sense of what is going on around you. You need to be aware of two critical elements:

- How you spend money, both consciously and unconsciously
- How others *want* you to spend your money

In the pages to come, you will have plenty of opportunities to become more aware of how you spend money. Right now we'd like to focus your attention on developing an awareness of how others *want* you to spend your money—a key element in the philosophy of living on a budget.

Every time we open a newspaper, flip through a magazine, glance at a passing bus, or watch television, we are exposed to extraordinary pressure from advertisers. Don't ever forget there's an entire huge industry—the marketing and advertising business— in which lots of smart people spend a lot of time sitting around in rooms trying to figure out new ways to entice you to spend money on things. Things that— gasp—you probably don't really need.

Much of the philosophy of living on a budget involves developing an awareness of all the commercial hype, and then intentionally tuning it out. Not only can you tune it out, but you also can eventually begin to feel quite superior to those mindless folks who still succumb to commercial messages. It's a delicious feeling!

123 **By the Numbers** _____

Jennifer's sister Anne lives in Chicago with her teenage son, Alex. A freelance writer, she tries to stretch her income as far as she can. When either she or Alex decides they really *must* have something new, they purposely delay the purchase a week. "In a week, you might well lose interest entirely," she says. "You prevent impulse buying. And the longer you reflect, the less you may find you need it."

Money See, Money Do

Also, you need to be aware of how much you and your spending are affected by the purchases of these folks:

- Your neighbors
- Your friends
- Your family

Find yourself falling into the "envy trap" more often than you'd like? Ah, we can see you blushing now! Don't worry, it affects all of us at one time or another—the burning desire to purchase a jet ski just because the one parked in the driveway next door looks so incredibly cool! Never mind that you can't swim, don't live near a large body of water, and don't know the first thing about how to drive one. It looks cool, so you must have one, too.

That fuzzy new sweater your office mate wore on Monday? One of those would be great. To heck with what the balance already is on your Nordstrom card!

Did you notice the food processor your Mom has? It has all those switches, the color matches her kitchen, and it has an incredible warranty! Of course you'll need one, no question about it.

As you can see, these folks can be dangerous. But we don't think you'll have to avoid them while you're trying to live on a budget. No, once again we just want you to be *aware* of the way their purchases can affect yours.

 **By the Numbers**

Financial writer and commentator Jane Bryant Quinn is a big fan of wise spending. She thinks that the only three reasons *not* to budget are (1) that you are rich enough to buy whatever you want and have plenty of other money left over, and (2) "I forgot the other two." Guess there really aren't any good reasons for not living on a budget!

Did we also mention "mindless"? Yes, we did say "mindless," because the opposite of awareness is mindlessness. Mindlessly plopping the credit card on the counter even though you might actually have enough cash in your pocket. Mindlessly going along with the idea that your kids will have a ghastly Christmas unless you brave the crowds and buy them a Nintendo DS/X Box/iPod/Fashion Barbie. Combat mindless spending! Develop your awareness; abandon your mindlessness.

Turn That TV Off Now!

Where does most of the mad impulse to spend come from, anyway? Some of us just seem to be born that way, with credit card in hand and a burning desire to purchase a pair of faux fur slippers *right now!* Sad to say, most of the desire originates on the outside—right there on a television screen, to be exact.

Television commercials used to get most of the blame for driving so many of us to go out and buy, buy, buy. But the finger of blame now points squarely to *the television shows themselves.* The research of Harvard University's Juliet B. Schor proves that. Because most television shows are set in the realm of the upper class or the very rich (can you picture the oh-so-perfect worlds of *Desperate Housewives* or *The OC*?), watching those shows actually makes people want to own some of the things shown on the screen, things few of us can really afford. Designer clothes and sleek cars from glitzy detective shows set us dreaming about the fast life. Perfectly matched living room furniture in the background of a family sitcom might make us cast a weary eye around our own living rooms and vow to upgrade to buttery tan leather upholstery.

Television commercials also create a longing for many things that the average household will never be able to afford and cause us to compare our lives, not with the folks in our same economic bracket, but the folks at the very top. As Juliet Schor explains in her book *The Overspent American*, "A major sporting event … is likely to deliver [for television advertisers] more millionaires than [an ad in *Forbes*] …. In the process, painters who earn $25,000 a year are being exposed to buying pressures never intended for them, and middle-class housewives look at products once found only in the homes of the wealthy."

Professor Schor's research showed that households with the highest viewing rates also had the lowest savings rates. How are you ever going to make it to the bank with your weekly savings deposit if you first have to make it past all those television commercials for more, better, newer stuff? It appears that most folks don't.

Unplug It Tonight!

So how do you combat commercial hype? Get up from your comfy couch, cross the room, and yank the plug! Sounds genuinely un-American to advocate watching less television, we know, and it might not be realistic for you and your family. Remember, we do understand that "crash diets" of any kind are doomed to fail.

But remember the point we've tried to make about how critical it is to be aware of the commercial messages you're receiving. The greater your awareness of how hard everyone is working to get you to part with some of your cash, the greater the chances are that you will hang on to it yourself!

Careful of the Glossy Pages

You should also be aware of the overwhelming advertising that assaults you every time you open a glossy magazine. Women's magazines aren't just full of perfume strips—they're also chock full of images that will make you feel far from perfect and satisfied until you … buy their product! They have page after page of advertising that will convince you your face is wrinkled (so buy their cream!), your wardrobe is inadequate (so buy their jeans!), and your thighs are jiggly (so buy their exerciser!). Read the articles, put those perfume strips in your underwear drawer as a free scented sachet, and ignore all other attempts to persuade you to purchase.

Above All, Know Thyself

Let's get back to the basic philosophy of budgeting. Another critical piece of the puzzle is the ability to Know Thyself, and while you're at it, to Know Thy Family. Before you sit down to draw up a budget that works, stop and think about the kind of stuff you are prone to buy now. Do you make the decision to buy because …

- You believe that the item is "the best," a real quality product that will last for years to come?
- You believe you deserve a "treat"?
- You believe that buying in quantity now (even if you don't need that much of whatever the item is) will get you a better price?

- You believe that if you don't buy it *now*, the price will just go up and you'll miss your chance?
- You think you absolutely need it (but can't really say why)?

Or maybe you're not really sure why you buy (one look at the jumble of stuff in your closet might be a good hint); you just do.

Let's also think about how well you can ...

- Keep track of numbers.
- Stick to your goals.
- Adapt to changes in your routine.
- Overcome your impulses.

Impulse spending is a major budget buster. The strategies we advise will help you avoid impulse spending—don't be a slave to advertisers! By trying to delay your purchases, by thinking and considering an item for a week, two weeks, or even a month, you might well find that the mood has passed, and that you still have the money you might have spent on it. Peter has been considering the purchase of an expensive band saw for a whopping three years! In the meantime, he's been using the neighbor's saw for free, and the price of a good band saw has been falling. The desire to buy one hasn't passed, but he has yet to march down to Home Depot to buy one. Maybe next month ....

Instead of thinking about living on a budget, why not just change the terminology? Think of the new program you're about to embark on as a "spending plan," because it's really just a way of spending more wisely.

But Isn't It Hard?

Budgeting is not hard. Let us repeat that—budgeting is not hard. Our system is so simple that you will quickly find it becoming second nature. You'll discover it's natural to use it. Can you remember to keep track of just five different types of expenses? Of course you can. You don't have to track your household expenses the way a corporate accountant tracks multimillion-dollar expenses; you don't need to track every penny you have.

Didn't get a good grade in math? Don't sweat it; this isn't calculus we're pushing here. Just a small bit of addition and subtraction, nothing your grade schooler can't help you with if you run into trouble. And if you have kids, you'll be setting them a good example.

But Isn't It Boring?

Is life on a budget boring? Far from it! Once you develop more awareness about where your money has been going (and where you want it to go in the future) it can become quite fascinating. You will take great pleasure in the feeling of mastery you develop as living on a budget becomes routine. And you will

look back with amusement at your formerly spend-
thrift ways. Spend an entertaining hour flipping
back through old check registers or credit-card
statements. You'll wonder what on Earth ever pos-
sessed you to toss your money around like that.

And it's fun to think of new ways to cut your spending
or new ways to have fun without going to the ATM
machine. You have no doubt read articles about the
frugal living movement of the past few years. These
are folks who have really taken living on a budget to
heart and devoted themselves to living with less, or
thinking of new uses for the stuff they already have.
Are they bored? We don't think so.

Do I Really Have to Write It Down?

Do budgets always have to be written down? For
the first few months, yes. We recommend tracking
your budget on paper (or computer) for a while
until you get the hang of it. Once you've mastered
the basics of your budget and adopted the philosophy of sticking to it, you might be able to ignore
your written records. Remember, this does not have
to be a chore. You will soon be comfortable with
the spending levels you've set for yourself and will
be able to live quite nicely within them.

As your authors, Peter and Jennifer confess to not
having written down a budget for the past decade
or so, but we know what our spending plan is and
that effectively limits excessive spending and keeps
things under control. And if asked, we could tell
you exactly how much we allow ourselves to spend

on each category. That's what living on a budget is all about.

Is it always easy to live on a budget? Sometimes we do fight the impulse to spend more than we know we should on certain categories. Jennifer's big weakness is books. Peter's is camera equipment. But when standing in the aisles of a bookstore trying to decide whether to splurge on a new hardcover, Jennifer will suddenly be reminded that she would rather take a vacation in the Spring, and she heads down the street to the library instead.

The Least You Need to Know

- To budget effectively, you must develop an awareness of how and when you spend.
- It's important to develop an awareness of how much television shows and commercials affect your spending habits.
- Develop a sensitivity to how much the purchases of your friends, neighbors, and family affect your own spending.
- Once you commit to living on a budget, you can take great delight in discovering new ways to cut costs.

Getting Ready

In This Chapter

- Outline your income patterns
- Establish personal and family financial goals
- Establish a long-term approach
- If it's not working—change it!

Okay, let's start working on that budget. This chapter and the next give you the basics you need to start living successfully on a budget—and seeing positive financial results. In Chapter 4, we break the process down to 12 steps, all of which you can handle with ease.

In this chapter, we start you out in search of answers to some important questions—how much do you make, and how much do you spend? With these two answers in place, you can begin to see how this program will work for you.

Know Your Income, and Know Your Expenses

Income and expenses. Two fairly simple words, but with the power to make grown folks tremble and weep. Let's look closely at the different types of income and how that affects designing your budget.

Do you get a steady paycheck on a weekly, biweekly, or monthly basis? Or is your income a bit more, uh, erratic? So many of us are self-employed nowadays, and we're all too familiar with that nerve-wracking wait for the latest check we are owed—while the bills keep coming.

What about the little dribs and drabs of income that sometimes show up in the mail without warning— a nice little birthday check from your great-aunt Mabel, the occasional bonus check as a reward for a job well done, or a fat dividend check from that stock you've owned for years?

All income? Yep, and it's all income that has to be taken into account while you're trying to get a handle on your finances. Let's start by drawing up a list of all the possible sources of income you have and how often you receive them.

Write the words "Total Income" at the top of a blank piece of paper and put it all down.

Should you also include tiny things like interest to checking accounts? We say skip it. Why risk feeling overwhelmed by having to track *every* last nickel and dime?

In One Hand and Out the Other

If only our lives consisted of receiving income. But alas, that income has to go out the door again in the form of expenses. So let's see what kinds of expenses you're dealing with.

There are three types of expenses you need to map out:

- Monthly expenses
- Quarterly expenses
- Annual expenses

Monthly expenses are the easiest to spot. Here we can lump together things like your rent or mortgage payment, car payments, most utilities, phones, and the now-ubiquitous online charges. Although monthly expenses vary somewhat, many of them (like mortgage or rent) are fixed, and many (such as utilities) don't vary too much from month to month.

Do you see something missing from the list of monthly expenses? Something quite large? Like perhaps your credit-card bills? Truth be told, however, credit-card bills are not an expense. Instead, they are just an expensive way to pay for something else, something that probably falls into another category.

Quarterly expenses are also largely fixed. They might be estimated tax payments, community-association dues, tuition payments, garbage and water charges, and most insurance payments.

Annual expenses can be anything from your yearly Christmas gift blowout to charitable giving. The size of some of your annual expenses might surprise you.

Financial Forensics

How do you dredge up all this info on expenses, anyway? By doing some detective work. Delve deep into your records. Start combing through desk drawers and dusty file folders for old checking account statements, credit-card statements, and ATM charges. Pay particular attention to those ATM withdrawals!

Classified Information

The information you've come up with so far about your income and expenses is quite valuable. In Chapter 4, we teach you how to classify these expenses and put together a spending plan that *works*.

Feeling sorry for yourself now that you've written down your income and expenses in black and white? Everything is just so *darned* expensive! Actually, just to help you put things in perspective, consider this: According to a global survey, the international rankings of the highest costs of living put Tokyo in first place, with London in second. The United States doesn't even show up on the list until New York in twelfth place, followed by Los Angeles in twenty-seventh, Chicago in thirty-fifth, and San Francisco in thirty-eighth place. Count your blessings you aren't working on this budget in Tokyo!

Budget Bombs

According to the banking industry, the average ATM withdrawal is $60. It seems like such a small sum but if you withdraw it once or twice a week you can bleed through your money without really knowing where you spent it. Try to wean yourself and your family members from the ATM machine, and limit weekly withdrawals.

Setting Goals

Setting goals is Jennifer's favorite topic. Peter is the man to see about the checkbook and income flow, but Jennifer is in charge of goals for the Sander family.

What do we mean by goals? You might have many kinds of goals for your life (to climb Mt. Everest, to be quoted in *The Wall Street Journal*, or to golf the perfect game at Pebble Beach), but within the context of this book, we'll stick to financial goals. Some good financial goals are building up a savings account, paying off a big credit card, or setting aside money for a summer vacation. Financial goals also include planned purchases or expenditures—your desire to someday have a home in the mountains or to build a well-equipped home office. Goal-setting is a wonderful way to pass a rainy afternoon, so let's get started on this one right away.

Do you want to share your goals with other people? If you do, you just might find that they are able to help you achieve those goals. "I posted a list of short-term goals on the wall of my apartment," Cathleen Swanson of Kenwood, California, told us. "I posted the list in a place where I could see it all the time, and it turned out that other folks noticed it, too. The list ranged from "acquire ironing board" to things like "washer and dryer." And a most remarkable thing happened—people started to offer up extra stuff that they had! So instead of having to buy that ironing board, I got a great used one from a friend who was moving. I even ended up with a washer and dryer that was nearly new. This could be a real budget-minded way to clear a few small items off of your short-term goals list!

You'll need three separate sheets of paper, one for *short-term goals*, one for *medium-term goals*, and one for *long-term goals*. If you're doing this with your spouse, you'll need six pieces of paper, because we want you each to work up your own goals list to begin with.

> **Moneywise Meanings**
>
> **Long-term goals**—Financial goals you plan to achieve in the next 5 to 20 years.
>
> **Medium-term goals**—Financial goals you'd like to achieve in the next 5 years.
>
> **Short-term goals**—Financial goals you plan to achieve in the next 12 months.

Particularly Pleasant Paperwork

Put pen to paper, and let your imagination get to work. What is it that you want to achieve financially? Don't feel shy or reticent about what your goals are. If what you really want is a big shiny boat, then put it down! Yes, we've poked a bit of fun in the last two chapters about what kinds of things people buy, but what we were trying to point out was that impulse buying wrecks a budget in a second. Put that boat down on paper as a long-term goal, and we will help you work up a budget plan to put it into your driveway!

Daydreams and Dollar Signs

Start writing down the kinds of long-term goals that come to mind. Long-term goals are going to be large expenditures, such as …

- Paying for the kids' college educations.
- Taking a six-month around-the-world vacation.
- Starting your own business.

Chances are that you will be able to come up with only three or four long-term goals. And that is wise; you don't want to split your efforts too much while working toward achieving them. A list of 20 long-term financial goals, each of which might require 20 or 30 thousand dollars or more, is really too daunting to tackle.

Having nailed down some long-term goals, move on to the longer list of things you'd like to accomplish in the next five years or so. Your medium-term goals might be things such as …

- Tuition for the night school MBA program.
- A three-week trip to the south of France.
- Adding a second story to the house.
- Buying a new Volvo station wagon.
- Sending Junior to summer camp every year.

Your short-term goals list might look something like this:

- Pay off credit cards.
- Save enough for a house down payment.
- Build up emergency savings reserves.
- Buy new ski equipment.
- Fix the car's air conditioner.
- Buy a new winter coat.

You will probably have twice as many—or even more!—short-term goals as medium- or long-term goals. Go ahead and put down as many as you'd like, but realize they won't all be accomplished in the same time period. How will they be accomplished, then? Rotation.

As your budget enables you to accomplish one of your short-term goals, you cross that one off and rotate another one to your list in its place. Let's say that in the first six months you set enough aside to buy both the new winter coat and the ski equipment. Great! Scratch those two off your list of short-term goals. No doubt you already have a few more in mind that you can now add to the list. The point is to keep the list of short-term goals you're working on manageable. Having too many big long-term financial goals is as much of a problem as having too many short-term goals. It can seem overwhelming and keep you from even trying.

Husbands and Wives Together

Finished with your lists of goals, both long and short-term? If you're working on those lists at one end of the kitchen table while your spouse works at the other end, it's time to get those six pieces of paper together. Pass your lists to each other and review them quietly, with an emphasis on "quietly." Don't laugh, ridicule, or otherwise comment on what your spouse has chosen to put on the goals list. Just as you want your goals to be taken seriously, treat your spouse's hopes and dreams with the same respect.

You will, however, need to negotiate a bit if your lists don't match. Decide together just what the long-term goals should be. You might need to compromise some of your short-term goals—for example, keeping one or two items (winter coat, ski equipment) that benefit only you, while your spouse adds a few items that he or she alone benefits from. Sound fair? Keep it that way.

Secrets of Successful Goal Setting

So much has been written about the awesome power of goal setting. Some motivational speakers and writers make claims that once you write down a goal, the universe will help you achieve it! Wow! We want the universe on our side, of course, but we have a somewhat more down-to-earth idea about why lists of goals work.

Just like a shopping list or a to-do list, when you commit something to paper, you feel duty-bound to complete it. This is not the universe working for you, just simple guilt compelling you to do what you've just decided you should do anyway. Other than your own guilt and built-in desire to not let yourself (or your family) down, here are a few other ways to make sure you can stick to accomplishing your short- and long-term goals:

- Keep the list of long-term goals manageable, just three or four (or less).
- Make sure your short-term financial goals are realistic and really can be accomplished within a short time period.
- Post the list where you and your family can keep an eye on it.
- Make reviewing your goals a family occasion, and make a big production out of accomplishing a goal (and crossing it off!).
- Don't resent your goals, or feel constrained by them; remember that you chose each and every one of them.

You and your family put a lot of thought and effort into creating your list of goals, so don't lose it in a back drawer now. Jennifer likes to review the Sander family's list of goals and check progress every Monday, but this might be excessive. You might decide to pull out your list on the first day of every month so that you can gear up to properly handling your finances that month. You will soon learn how often you need to check your list to stay on track.

The "Lifestyle" Issue

Now that you're starting to get a clearer idea of just where your money (and how much of it) goes on a monthly basis, there's one other factor we would like you to consider. In many instances, you made a conscious decision to commit money to something that is … costly. Perhaps you and your family decided to buy the house with a mortgage of $2,500 a month, and get the car that costs $400 a month, and participate in the annual Christmas gift-giving extravaganza. The lifestyle you've chosen comes with a price tag.

Compare some of your fixed monthly expenses to your long-term financial goals. Does your desire to live in that house outweigh your desire to someday spend six months wandering around the world? Does the pleasure you take in driving that car outweigh the pleasure you would get from running your own business? Hmmm … it could be that the answer to achieving some of your long-term goals sooner lies in adjusting some of your lifestyle choices. End of our lecture—these decisions are *yours* to make.

All Those in Favor, Say "Aye"

One of the critical factors in successful budgeting is making sure everyone in your family is on board 100 percent—and not just the folks who carry around checkbooks and credit cards. Your kids need to be with the program, too.

Just as it was important that you and your spouse agreed on what the long-, medium-, and short-term goals should be, it's important that everyone agrees to *stick to the budget*.

You need to be in agreement about what everyone will gain from changing the way your family finances are run.

Sticking with the Plan

Once you have commitment and agreement, is there anything else you'll need? Yes, actually. Two words: wisdom and discipline.

Wisdom? Yes, wisdom. The wisdom to see that not buying that expensive bauble in the mail-order catalog will make you richer in the long run. The wisdom to know that even if you envy the fancy toys your neighbor seems able to afford, you have made conscious decisions about how you're going to gain control of your finances.

And discipline? Discipline is key. We won't kid you; it does take discipline to stick to any kind of spending plan. Our plan has built-in allowances and treats, but it's far from the free-spending lifestyle you might have enjoyed up to now. It takes discipline to budget your money, but we believe that you have that discipline. Heck, if *we* can stick to a budget, *anyone* can!

This Isn't Working? Change It!

What if you find that the budget you draw up is a bit too ... tight? Just too difficult to live with? Well, then you might have to adjust it. There's no sense trying to force yourself to stick to a plan you're constantly busting out of. Better to change it, to have a budget that more accurately reflects your lifestyle, than to fail. But realize that it might put your goals even further out of sight. You will have to decide which is more important.

What a Big Stack of Paper!

By now, you should have a few pieces of paper floating around:

- A complete list of your income sources and amounts
- A complete list of your expenses, broken down monthly, quarterly, and yearly
- A list of long-term goals
- A list of medium-term goals
- A list of short-term goals

Congratulations! You've worked hard to uncover all that info. Now what should you do with it? Put it in a neat pile, and turn to the next chapter.

The Least You Need to Know

- You must be aware of exactly what your income is from all sources.

- Uncover all expenses and sort them into monthly, quarterly, and annual categories to understand your cash needs.

- Take the time to set financial goals—long-term, medium-term, and short-term—that sticking to a budget can help you achieve.

- All family members need to be committed to living within the budget plan.

- If your plan is failing, better to fix it than to abandon it altogether.

The Twelve Steps to Pulling It Off

In This Chapter

- Grouping expenses to make sense of them
- Anticipating regular bills
- Setting up your four savings funds
- Examining your take-home pay

You're making steady progress here. You know a little more about yourself—your goals, your habits (good and bad), and your personal financial situation. You also know some of the basic principles of budgeting, and we've told you that it isn't as painful as you thought. Now it's time to put it all to work (and, we hope, make good on our promise about that "it isn't as painful as you thought" part).

We will help you build a budget from the ground up. Not brick by brick (remember, this is a *Pocket Idiot's Guide*), but wall by wall, so to speak. You'll lay out some figures, see the result, and then go back and rip out a few pieces and reinsert new numbers if you have to.

Why? Because few budgets come out perfect the first time through. (If it does, you probably didn't need a budget in the first place. Either you're filthy rich, or you knew your finances better than you thought!) Squeeze here, add a little there, and *voilà*.

Remember the goal: use wisdom and discipline to achieve a positive financial (and emotional!) balance at the end of each month—or at least *most* months ....

So let's get started!

You're a Third of the Way Home

What? A *12-step* formula for budgeting? The last time you had to follow a 12-step procedure it was to remove the entire front end of your Honda to replace a headlight, and you swore you'd never do that again. Well, we have two pieces of good news for you:

- The end result is a lot more rewarding than a working headlight.
- You've already completed the first four steps!

Here's what you've already accomplished (in Chapter 3):

1. **Understand your income.** You know where your money comes from and your financial peaks and valleys through the year.

2. **Understand your expenses.** Ahh ... the "financial forensics"—digging into every nook and cranny to capture the essence of your monthly, quarterly, and yearly expenses.

3. **Set goals.** Remember all that stuff about short-term, medium-term, and long-term goals? Talking it over with your spouse in the context of your newly acquired income and expense enlightenment? If you really did do this, you're in great position to move forward.

4. **Understand your habits and situation.** It's much ado about where you spend, how you spend, and who in your family spends.

The Next Steps

Okay, so now you're a *little* relieved that you've gotten credit for completing the first four steps. But what about the next eight? Well, if you did a good job with 1 through 4, then 5 through 12 should come easy. If you left a lot of holes, well .... It might not be a bad idea to go back and read through Chapter 3 again.

Let's take a little trip through steps 5 to 12:

5. **Get savings and spending mechanisms in place.** Create the proper savings and reserves setup, acquire low-interest credit cards and a free checking account, and put your money "on the tracks" and keep it running.

6. **Plan your income.** Now that you know your income sources and their timing, you can lay out an income plan.

7. **Plan your obligations.** These are the "must-pays," such as mortgage, rent, insurance, property taxes, car payments, and the like.

8. **Plan your necessities.** These are the "consumable" items and expenses, such as food, utilities, and basic maintenance expenses.

9. **Set aside pocket money.** This is the spending money for daily and weekly incidentals, such as lunches, coffee, snacks, and video rentals.

10. **Create a family allowance.** This is where your family spending goals are covered, as well as recreation, entertainment, and routine outings.

11. **Create a personal allowance.** Your "PAL" is discretionary money that you alone can spend to meet goals or for whatever you want.

12. **Balance and rebalance.** Most often your budget doesn't come out the way you want—not enough to meet your goals or give you an adequate family or personal allowance. Push and pull, and come up with a plan that achieves an acceptable balance. Remember, *you* are in charge!

Now, as we go through these steps (we discuss steps 5 and 6 in this chapter, steps 7 through 11 in Chapter 5, and step 12 in Chapter 6), you'll notice that it isn't as hard as it sounds. We won't make you budget for every 69¢ soda you buy at the gas station! You will simply learn to simplify so that you have adequate limits and you maintain those limits. Spend it however you like, but keep it within the limit!

More to Think About

What about the time horizon for steps 5 and 6? Like most people, you probably need a monthly budget, but not all months are created equal! So to create a good monthly budget, we have to plan weekly, monthly, quarterly, yearly, and other income and expenses.

And what about savings? The prudent budgeter uses savings for a lot more than just a retirement nest egg. In Chapter 7, you'll learn the use of special types of savings to s-m-o-o-o-t-h the bumps in the budget roller coaster.

And the Category Is ...

To try to make things simpler, for steps 7 through 11 we group expenses into categories to make them easier to manage. The categories are roughly determined by the level of discretion—that is, choices—you can make about how much you spend on what.

You'll learn to recognize and plan for expenses in each of five categories—obligations, necessities, pocket money, family, and personal allowances. Separate categories for "sodas in gas stations" and "athletic socks" just aren't necessary.

Save Right, Spend Right, for Retirement

"Oh, no, not another boring book about how to save for retirement!" Indeed not. In the context of budgeting, yes, retirement savings are one element that you should budget for. But in Chapter 6 we focus on savings as a tool to help you live on a budget. The kind of savings we're talking about never grow long term. They are simply used to smooth out the bumps in your annual budget cycle.

Credit Cards

Is there a right way and a wrong way to use credit cards and checking accounts? Credit cards can be financial death, and every budgeting book talks about the dangers of overusing them. Sorry, we will, too (in Chapter 7).

But credit cards, while *often* the most expensive way to pay for something, are sometimes the best way to manage certain expenses (more about this in Chapter 7).

Saving Your $$: Step 5

Time to get started on step 5—getting savings and spending mechanisms in place. Let's talk about four types of savings, or personal "funds": *income reserve fund, obligation* or *"must" fund, contingency* or *"rainy day" fund,* and *leisure* or *"want" fund.* These savings pigeonholes can be separate savings accounts or can be grouped for simplicity, or they can be envelopes of cash in your medicine cabinet! (It's been done, but we don't really recommend it.)

- **Income reserve fund.** For those of you whose income is irregular, we recommend a carefully managed, highly visible savings (or investment) account to park your funds in during the high times of your income cycle— "park" so you have funds you need during financially dry times, and "visible" so you can carefully manage and plan your future. Avoid at all costs the temptation to go out and spend that commission check the same month you get it.

  For those of you who own small businesses, a practical way to save your income is simply to keep it in your business. Only draw what you need when you need it, and keep track of the owner's equity account as though it were a savings account.

- **Obligation or "must" fund.** These are savings designed to meet expenses that you know will come up during the year, but that don't always occur monthly, such as property taxes and most types of insurance. If you have a $600 car insurance payment due twice a year, that payment could be a budget buster during the two months it comes due.

Savvy budgeters set aside $100 a month in their "must" fund. For those of you who are homeowners, this is sort of like an "impound" account often used by mortgagers to ensure property tax and homeowner's insurance payments. Extra credit goes to those who have it deducted from their paycheck and *automatically* saved in the "must" fund account.

123 By the Numbers

As a professional writer and book packager, Jennifer gets paid only three or four times a year. At first this pattern really wreaked havoc with our budget. Sometimes she had quite a bit of money in the bank, and sometimes she had nothing at all! How did we smooth it out? Instead of just depositing her checks into our regular checking account, we set up a separate account to make it easy to track the balance, tax payments, and expenditures. Before we did this, we dealt with some unpleasant budgetary and tax surprises.

So what is the benefit of setting up a "must" fund? Aside from peace of mind, take the following example. Our car insurance totals $1,200 per year, due twice a year in $600 installments. The insurance company offers a monthly payment plan to smooth out the payments, but charges $5 per month to do so. By using a must fund instead, not only do we save 60 bucks (the cost of a pretty nice dinner), but we also collect interest on the savings—only about $9 per year at today's low interest rates, but hey ... it pays for the tip!

Savvy Saver

Try to plan far enough ahead to treat your charitable contributions and gift-giving plans as obligations and "impound" to meet them. Also, having mortgage payments made automatically keeps this money from reaching your hands—and getting spent.

- **Contingency or "rainy day" fund.** Car repairs, medical expenses, and fixing that leaky roof are examples of the myriad budget busters that can happen during the year. Nobody is immune from these events; it's all part of life as usual. What you *should* do, however, is set aside part of your income in a special contingency fund to handle these emergencies. We recognize that it's hard to plan for all of them, but looking at your past financial record should help. Again, you get extra credit if you have this money taken off the top and automatically set aside.

123 By the Numbers _____

Peter learned about setting up a leisure fund from his parents, Jerry and Betty. Every week they stashed another $20 or $40 into their vacation fund, saving up throughout the year to pay cash for their annual road trip out west. He remembers the thrill he felt as a child when the cash box was finally opened and the fruits of the year's savings were counted out in careful stacks—it seemed like a fortune!

- **Leisure or "want" fund.** Sounds like retirement, eh? Well, not quite. We recognize that everyone needs to relax, take vacations, and spend a little time and money on recharging the batteries. The right way to do so is to set up yet another account that you pay into each month. If you don't, we _know_ what happens. You decide you need the vacation anyway, and out comes the MasterCard (we've seen the commercials, too). You consume today, and your suntan fades before the first payment is due. Now it takes a year or more to pay the thing off, with interest in the hundreds of dollars. Think of the nice dinners you could have bought with the interest savings (and interest earned) if you'd only set it aside in advance! As a practical matter, this savings can be combined with one of your other accounts. But for starters especially, it's probably a good idea to set it up separately.

How Many Dang Accounts Do I Need?

So are we saying that each of these types of savings should be in a separate account? You'd need to add on to your house just to be able to store all that extra info.

No, you don't need a bunch of different accounts, but you do need to write down *somewhere* just how much of what you have in your big savings account goes where. If one week you want to add $50 to your vacation fund, for example, write it down, and if you add $100 the next week to your contingency fund, write that down, too. At any given time, you'll know that your savings account of, say, $3,500 is apportioned as follows:

- $1,000 earmarked for the contingency fund
- $1,500 earmarked for the "must" fund
- $1,000 earmarked for your next vacation

Check It Out

So you really can use just one savings account. What about checking accounts? Do you need more than one? We think one checking account is all that's necessary for most single folks and for most families. Checking accounts can be expensive. They come with all kinds of charges and pitfalls, so why not just keep track of one?

Incoming! Step 6

Let's move on to step 6, planning your income. You've already figured out last year's income stream, or at least the important parts—Aunt Maude's birthday check and the interest on your checking account excluded. Now you need to lay out a plan for the next 12 months. Should it resemble last year's plan, or shouldn't it? Let's use it as a place to start.

Income can be separated into gross, take-home, and available categories:

- *Gross income* is simply your gross pay, or salary, if you're employed by someone else. It can be a regular salary, or an irregular one in the form of commission, bonus payments, or some combination of the two. Of course, you never see this figure because of taxes and other deductions.

- *Take-home income* is the amount that actually makes it into your paycheck and into your checking account. Items like federal, state, and local income taxes, FICA (Social Security and Medicare), and the like are taken out. This isn't a tax book, so we aren't going to delve into withholding strategies, but we do recommend withholding what you think you need or just a little more (a tax refund can be a nice way to buy something you want or need without creating a budget bomb).

- *Available income* is what you make available for normal monthly expenses. It's what's left after you follow our recommendations and set aside a "must" fund, a "rainy day" fund, a "want" fund, and, as things get better, growth and retirement savings.

If you have a fixed monthly salary, your situation is relatively simple. If your income is irregular, however, you need to set up an income-management plan that includes an income-reserve account. Take-home and available income will be outcomes of this plan, with the income-reserve account used to smooth out the bumps.

What the heck are we talking about? Let's look at some completely fictitious financial folks: Lilly the Librarian and Sam the Sales Rep. Numbers in parentheses are subtracted.

Lilly the Librarian:	
Salary	$36,000/year or $3,000/month
Gross pay	$3,000
Less taxes, FICA, disability, etc.	($900)

Take-home pay	$2,100
Less obligation savings	($200)
Contingency savings	($100)
Leisure savings	($100)
	========
Available income	$1,700

Sam the Sales Rep:	
Salary (draw)	$12,000
Plus commissions ranging from 0 (low season) to $8,000/month in the spring and early summer	
Total commissions last year	$24,000
Gross pay	$36,000/year
Gross pay per month	$3,000
Less taxes, FICA, disability, etc.	($900)

Take-home pay	$2,100
Less obligation savings	($200)
Contingency savings	($100)
Leisure savings	($100)
	========
Available income	$1,700

Why are we showing you two people who make the same income? The difference between Sam and Lilly is that Sam must set aside some or all of those $8,000 monthly commissions in an income-management savings account. The upshot is that *both* have $1,700 of available income per month. Remember that we might make a repeat trip or two through these numbers, adjusting must fund, rainy day fund, and want fund savings to make ends meet.

Stepping Out with Your Money

Okay, let's review steps 5 and 6. You're getting a clearer picture of how setting up different types of savings funds can help you live a smoother, less tumultuous financial life. No more scrambling to find extra cash to fix the car—you budgeted for that. No more last-minute scrimping to pay the property tax bill—it was in the budget and you've got the cash. As long as you keep some sort of written record of which money is earmarked for what, one main savings account is all that's necessary.

From the examples of Lilly and Sam, we can see that it's best to take this money right off the top, out of the take-home pay. Now, what are we planning to do with the rest of that paycheck? Read on to the next chapter and see how to budget for rent, food, and even fun!

The Least You Need to Know

- Few budgets come out perfect the first time; it takes a lot of tinkering to get them right.

- Most people need a monthly budget, but you must also budget for large semiannual bills, such as insurance payments or property taxes.

- The four types of savings are income reserve funds, obligation funds, contingency funds, and leisure funds.

- Only one actual savings account is necessary, but you must have a handle on how much money is earmarked for what.

- Whether your income is regular or irregular will affect your budgeting plan.

The Last Few Steps

In This Chapter

- Separating your "must-pay" obligations
- Putting food on the table
- Keeping money in your side pocket
- Establishing a family allowance

You're well on your way now. Six steps down, and six to go. You already have a handle on your past income and expenses and your future goals. You've already set up wise methods for spending and saving, and you've started your budget by outlining an income plan. Where to now? Get the expenses down, create some allowances, and make some adjustments. Then you're done preparing ... and it's time to live, time to play!

Recall the last six steps from Chapter 4:

7. Plan your obligations.
8. Plan your necessities.
9. Set aside pocket money.
10. Create a family allowance.

11. Create a personal allowance.

12. Balance and rebalance.

On to budgeted expenses.

Much Obliged: Step 7

The first category (step 7) is to "plan your obligations," or must-pays. As Chapter 4 pointed out, these expenses are controllable in the long run, depending on lifestyle choices you make. In the short run, they are big expenses that must be budgeted for. Some, such as property taxes or car insurance, might be paid only a few times a year on a predictable schedule. Managing them means making sure they are in the budget and paid on time. When you get there, you've accomplished step 7!

What to include on your must-pay list:

- Mortgage or rent
- Homeowner's or renter's insurance
- Property taxes
- Day care or child expenses
- Existing car payments
- Annual professional dues (for example, union dues)

Not sure what else belongs on this list? We'll give you an extensive list in Appendix A.

Remember to find *all* the must-pays and get them on paper. No two individuals or families are alike. And remember, no sense cheating—like everything else, and especially in budgeting, you're only cheating yourself!

Savvy Saver _____

The real trick to managing obligations is to (1) get them on paper, and (2) make them as routine as possible. You should never have to sweat over a mortgage or rent check. To make sure of that, you can use a must-pay savings reserve to collect this money from your paycheck automatically before it has a chance to disappear. Or you can have mortgage payments deducted automatically from your paycheck so you never touch the money at all!

Let's see how budgeting for must-pays works. Take a look at the way our friends Lilly the Librarian and Sam the Sales Rep budget their must-pays:

Lilly the Librarian

Must-Pay Item	Monthly Cost
Rent	$800
Car payment	$275

continues

Lilly the Librarian   (continued)

Must-Pay Item	Monthly Cost
Car insurance, $450 twice/year ($450 × 2 = $900/year; divide by 12 to get monthly amount)	$75

TOTAL OBLIGATIONS	$1,150

Sam the Sales Rep

Must-Pay Item	Monthly Cost
Mortgage	$500
Property tax, $600 twice/year ($600 × 2 = $1,200/year; divide by 12)	$100
Homeowner's insurance $480/year	$40
Day care	$300
Car payment	$200
Professional dues $120/year	$10

TOTAL OBLIGATIONS	$1,150

Food on the Table: Step 8

Now you know how much you need to keep a roof over your head, but what about the rest of your life? Let's start to capture the costs of "necessities," or consumable items and expenses that maintain the lifestyle you've chosen—food, utilities, medical expenses, home maintenance, gas, car maintenance, pest control, and so forth. You've decided that these items are all necessary (or if not, then it's a good time to do something about it now).

What to include on your necessities list:

- Groceries
- Utilities
- Phone
- Gas
- Medical expenses
- Home maintenance
- Pest control
- Cable TV
- School lunches and supplies
- And much, much more, depending on your situation

Appendix A has a much more extensive list for the "necessities" category.

Choices Make the Difference

Unlike the must-pay category, you can decide how, where, and when to spend your necessities expenses. Smart shopping and smart consumption come into play here to make the budget go further. How can you control all these budget items? By using simple common sense.

If you buy top-of-the-line cuts of beef, high-priced convenience foods, and bottles of swank wine at the grocery store, you will spend more in that category than the diligent guy who shops only the outer aisles (where all the fresh stuff is, no prepackaged foods).

If you send your kids off to school with a bologna sandwich and an apple, you're spending less than the parent who reaches for the "Lunchables" ready-made package.

If the lights burn brightly in your home at all hours and the heat is cranked way up, your utilities bill will indeed be higher than the folks who turn the light off when they leave the room and wear a sweater indoors, when necessary.

So yes, you do have control over this part of your budget, and the more attention you pay to it, the more control you can exert. With your efforts, the size of these budget items could well dwindle over time.

Savvy Saver

For an affordable night out, we like to head to a bar across from the California State Capitol that serves dinner. The chance of an Arnold-sighting adds a thrill, but so does the size of our modest bill. We each have a nice glass of Scotch, and then split a large prime rib dinner. Restaurant servings come so big nowadays that it is easy to feed two for the price of one!

Many of your small expenses are paid out bit by bit and can be a hassle to keep track of. There are a lot of ways to pay for gas for your car and other small expenses—out of pocket, with a check, with an ATM card, or with a credit card. To make it easier in the future, we recommend that you and your family pick which method suits you best and stick to it to help you track expenses.

Incorporating Necessities into the Budget

We'll make this easier for ourselves (and you!) by getting rid of Sam the Sales Rep and focusing on Lilly the Librarian. Not that we don't like ol' Sam; it's just that the two situations from here on are pretty much the same.

When you're done with this, you've nailed step 8! Here are Lilly's list of necessities:

Lilly the Librarian

Necessities Item	Monthly Cost
Groceries	$300
Utilities	$120
Phone	$50
Gas	$50
Medical expenses	
Home maintenance	$75
Pest control	
Cable TV	
School lunches/supplies	

TOTAL NECESSITIES	$595

One-Liners: Steps 9, 10, and 11

What's that, you say? This was supposed to be easy, and so far you've been hit with lists and lists of numbers? Well, that part is out of the way now. You have a good idea of how much your obligations and necessities—your lifestyle—set you back. We just had to get into detail. Why? Because these items represent a large portion of your budget (we know you knew that!). More to the point: the dangers of overlooking or underestimating them outweigh the convenience of simplifying.

Now it's time, in steps 9, 10, and 11, to set aside some funds for *you and your family*. We're going to keep this simple. For each of the next three budget items—and budget steps—we're going to deal with one-liners. We call them one-liners because you are going to deal with only *one* number for each category!

This is where we depart from much of the other literature on the subject of budgeting. One number, and one number only. We don't care how, where, or why you spend it, so long as you keep track and don't go over the limit.

Setting Aside Pocket Money: Step 9

Unless you're living in the Antarctic (does Domino's deliver there?), your travels through ordinary life take you past dozens of opportunities to spend your pocket money on all kinds of incidentals. Snacks, newspapers, magazines, fast food, pizza, movie rentals, tolls, parking .... If you're like most people, you "go to the wall" for this money—the ubiquitous ATM machine. When you run out, you go for more. Pretty soon, your checking account balance has nary a digit to the left of the decimal point.

What to include on your list of out-of-pocket expenses:

● Anything you want!

Again, here's where we depart from a lot of other budgeting and personal finance books. Don't bother trying to figure out a budget for each of these "knick knacks" of life. Simply set aside a certain amount of money (multiples of $20 are easy to work with) each week, and withdraw that amount from the ATM on a set day of the week. Monday is usually better than Friday for those who work a normal five-day week, as $20 bills have a tendency to burn holes in pockets on weekends. Rely on your wisdom and discipline.

Whatever the amount and timing, make it a routine and a ritual. If you don't, your finances usually careen out of control $20 at a time, and who hasn't been there? We don't care how you spend it; just don't go over. Finally, if expenses in this category go much over $10 per expenditure, this may be the wrong category.

Pocket money is discretionary, which means it might have to be trimmed if your budget doesn't balance. It may be hard to eliminate a lot of these expenses (we don't recommend skipping lunch at work, for example), but a little prudence could get a weekly allowance reduced from $60 to $40 per person.

> **Savvy Saver** _____
>
> Back in high school, Peter learned the word *Taschengeld* in his German class. It literally translates into "pocket money." He's used the term ever since so that he doesn't confuse his Taschengeld with any other item in our budget. And yes, Jennifer uses it, too!

Incidentally, how much money can Lilly the Librarian afford for these incidentals? About $40/week or $180/month for her to spend however the heck she wants, for starters.

Allow in the Family: Step 10

Now you have a roof over your head, food on the table, and a little pocket money to help you in the journey through life. Have we left out a few things? You bet. You haven't entertained yourself one iota or gotten out of the house.

You haven't bought anything to make your life easier, more enjoyable, or more rewarding, or to express your individuality.

Sound like a lot of stuff could be budgeted into this category? Nope. The same principle applies here as with step 9. Just pick a number and stick to it.

As with pocket money, you can include anything you want in this category. Having said that (again), here are some ideas for what this allowance should cover:

- Eating out, ice cream, and so on
- Going to the movies
- Family sports and recreation, such as golf, diving, boating trips, and so forth
- Outings—a day in the country
- Film, photofinishing, videos
- Gardening, minor home-improvement supplies
- Home decorating items
- Family gifts

Again, line-by-line analysis and budgeting isn't required for this step. We suggest setting aside a figure that feels right. Put it into the budget and see if it works. Do ends meet? If not, you may have to revisit the size of your family allowance. Remember the watchwords—wisdom and discipline.

This allowance is another "discretionary" expense, more discretionary than pocket money. You can get through life without most of these things, so in times of need, this is where you cut back first to make other ends meet. Or, if there's good news at the end of step 11 (your personal allowance—see below), you can add things you *really* want to do!

We don't recommend including family vacations in this category. They are too expensive and need to be more carefully planned for over the course of the year. For more on "leisure savings" see Chapter 4.

> **Savvy Saver**
>
> Since what *is* important is keeping track of your money, we recommend getting a separate credit-card account, with one card for each adult family member, that is used only for these items. This card is used *only* for expenses in this category.

How does Lilly do in this category? We'll start Lilly the Librarian with a monthly family allowance of $200.

Your Best PAL: Step 11

You're still feeling a little frustrated because you earn all that money and can't spend it on yourself. And what's more, you're still naked! No clothing in the budget so far! We talk about pocket money, and you have no pockets! Outrageous!

Not to worry (or shiver). Clothing and other personal "effects" and expenses are handled by yet another one-liner allowance account—your Personal Allowance, or PAL.

But isn't clothing one of the three basic necessities? Why save it for last in one of the *most* discretionary budget categories?

For most of us, clothing isn't bought as a strict necessity (with the exception of work uniforms) but as an enhancement to our self-image. We don't mean to be psychoanalytical here; we're just pointing out that clothing expenses are discretionary and personal by nature. So don't budget for three shirts, two pairs of shoes, half a dozen socks, and a suit for the next year. Just use *wisdom and discipline* to create a personal allowance, and be done with it!

Do you need both a family allowance and a PAL? If you're a family or a married couple, you definitely need *both* a family allowance and a PAL. If you're single, maybe not. You could combine, or you could (probably should) still keep them separate. Different items, different categories.

Include the following items in your PAL.

- Clothing
- Hobby expenses
- Personal recreation (gas for jet ski)
- Books, CDs
- Small consumer electronics
- Luggage
- Personal gifts
- A night out with friends

Check out the longer list of PAL items in Appendix A.

Month of January	Item	Balance	
GROSS GROSS		$ 3,000	
income reserve savings	$ 0		
GROSS		$ 3,000	
less payroll taxes, FICA	$ 800		
TAKE HOME		$ 2,200	
SAVINGS:			
must fund	$ 0		
rainy day fund	$ 0		
want fund	$ 0		
growth fund	$ 0		
retirement	$ 0		
TOTAL	$ 0		
AVAILABLE		$ 2,200	
MUSTS:			
mortgage/rent	$ 500		
property/renters insurance			$120 ONCE/YEAR
property taxes			
property dues or fees			
day care or tuition			
existing car payments	$ 195		
car insurance			$450 TWICE/YEAR
professional dues etc.			
TOTAL MUSTS:	$ 695		
SPENDABLE		$ 1,505	
NECESSITIES			
groceries	$ 250		
utilities	$ 120		
phone	$ 50		
gas	$ 50		
medical expenses			
school, lunches, expenses	$ 40		
home maintenance			
dry cleaning	$ 40		
pest control			
cable TV	$ 30		
TOTAL NECESSITIES:	$ 580		
DISCRETIONARY		$ 925	
POCKET MONEY	$ 180		
		$ 745	
FAMILY DISCRETIONARY			
FAMILY ALLOWANCE	$ 200	$ 545	
PERSONAL DISCRETIONARY			
PERSONAL ALLOWANCE	$ 200		
BALANCE		$ 345	

Lilly the Librarian's starting budget.

The key to putting your PAL into practice is to set a limit and stick to it. Set up a separate credit-card account with your name, for you only, and use it only for personal expenses. If you don't have an accountant's mind, write down your purchases during the month. Call the credit-card company if you lose track of how much you've spent. Don't go over the limit, and your PAL will be your best friend!

How does Lilly the Librarian fare here? We'll start out by giving Lilly a PAL of $200 per month.

Is your head swimming from all of this? Take a look at this simple chart for Lilly's budget on the previous page and see how it all falls together.

And That's It?

Yes, that's all there is to constructing a simple budget. Let's review the final steps:

7. Plan your obligations.
8. Plan your necessities.
9. Set aside pocket money.
10. Create a family allowance.
11. Create a personal allowance.
12. Balance and rebalance.

Hey, you caught us. Where did step 12 go? Right here, of course, at the very end. Because in the end, the budget you construct will either work with your income, or it won't. You have to rebalance, redesign, and rework the numbers until you find the right mix for you and your family. It may take a few months of tweaking before you perfect your own formula. When you hit on the right combo, however, your life and your finances will smooth out immediately! The next chapter covers budget-tweaking with step 12, so read on.

The Least You Need to Know

- Carefully list all your "must-pay" (obligation) expenses, such as mortgage, car payments, and property taxes, and budget so that you are never caught short for any of these large items.

- Draw up a list of consumable items and expenses like groceries, utilities, and cable TV bills.

- Recognize that, unlike most "must-pay" expenses, you can control how much you spend on these consumables by your shopping habits.

- Don't force yourself to live without a little money to carry around in your pockets, or you will fail in your budgeting.

- If your budget isn't working, pocket money and personal allowance are the first places to cut.

The Balancing Act

In This Chapter

- Developing budget worksheets
- Accounting for assets
- Reaching retirement with ease
- Budgeting for big "wants"

Are we done yet? This was supposed to be simple. Yet here we are, 5 chapters and 11 steps later, and it still isn't clear whether you'll need a second job at McDonald's to make ends meet. This chapter brings it all together, illustrating how a budget is constructed and put on paper. But that's not all. We still have to do step 12—balance and rebalance— to make sure your money goes where you want it to go. Now we create the plan—finally.

Getting It on Paper

No doubt you've been writing some things down while doing steps 1 through 11, so we won't go through it again here. Let's cut to the chase and see where we are. We'll ask Lilly, our cooperative librarian friend, to help us again. To add some realism to the example, we'll assume that Lilly is a single mom with one young son, Willy. Willy brings his own expenses and the need for a family allowance.

What's the best way to record a budget? Back of a napkin? Accountant's green sheets? A stone tablet? Omigosh—a computer? Answer: whatever works best for you. It's doubtful that the end result will ever be seen by anyone but you and perhaps a few involved family members. Neatness means little; accuracy and the ability to carry out the plan mean a lot more.

Having said that, computers *can* make the task a lot easier! A simple spreadsheet program, such as Microsoft Excel, MS Works, or Lotus 1-2-3 can make the budgeting task a lot easier. If you change a number, the effects are immediately visible, and you can enter "actuals" during the month to track how well you're doing.

There are also specialized programs, such as Quicken's Intuit, that "package" the budgeting process even more and can be excellent ways to get started and keep it going. But you don't *need* a computer to live on a budget!

The Life of Lilly the Librarian

Let's take a look at the first of seven worksheets:

Month of January				
		Item		Balance
GROSS GROSS			$	**3,000**
	income reserve savings	$ 0		
GROSS			$	**3,000**
	less payroll taxes, FICA	$ 800		
TAKE HOME			$	**2,200**
	SAVINGS:			
	must fund	$ 0		
	rainy day fund	$ 0		
	want fund	$ 0		
	growth fund	$ 0		
	retirement	$ 0		
	TOTAL	$ 0		
AVAILABLE			$	**2,200**
	MUSTS:			
	mortgage/rent	$ 500		
	property/renters insurance			$120 ONCE/YEAR
	property taxes			
	property dues or fees			
	day care or tuition			
	existing car payments	$ 195		
	car insurance			$450 TWICE/YEAR
	professional dues etc			
	TOTAL MUSTS:	$ 695		
SPENDABLE			$	**1,505**
	NECESSITIES			
	groceries	$ 250		
	utilities	$ 120		
	phone	$ 50		
	gas	$ 50		
	medical expenses			
	school, lunches, expenses	$ 40		
	home maintenance			
	dry cleaning	$ 40		
	pest control			
	cable TV	$ 30		
	TOTAL NECESSITIES:	$ 580		
DISCRETIONARY			$	**925**
POCKET MONEY		$ 180		
			$	745
FAMILY DISCRETIONARY				
	FAMILY ALLOWANCE	$ 200	$	545
PERSONAL DISCRETIONARY				
	PERSONAL ALLOWANCE	$ 200		
BALANCE			$	**345**

Lilly the librarian's starting budget.

What Have We Here?

Let's look at Lilly's budget for the month of January. What do we (or should we) notice?

- No income reserve—Lilly's income is paid in even monthly checks through the year, so no reserve is necessary. If Lilly had extraordinary or irregular income in January that had to cover for other months, this item would have a dollar figure.

- Death and taxes—For most of us, death isn't a budget item, but taxes must be taken care of. You can find this number by looking at your paycheck's withholding amounts.

- What, no savings?—We'll get to that. We begin at the starting point, and then go back and fill in savings goals appropriately.

- Un-monthly musts—As we look at the list of "must" expenses, we see two that aren't even in the numbers. Both insurances are billed less often than monthly, so we made a note at the side. Guess where they'll go? In the "must fund" savings that will cover them in the month when they *are* due. We'll get to that in a second.

- More than halfway—By the time you pay taxes, musts, and necessities, you've used up more than two thirds of your money. You have no savings, and life isn't any fun yet. Stick around ….

- Discretion is the better part of budgeting— Now here come the discretionary expenses.

Just for starters, there's $180 in pocket money, $200 in family allowance, and $200 in personal allowance. Nice round numbers. All those little family outings, movies, ice cream, some clothing—*covered*!

● Yippee, we're positive!—True, there's $345 left over at the end of the month, but it isn't time to pick up the mail-order catalogs just yet. We have to fund the must fund, contingency fund, and want funds. We have to retire someday, and we might actually want to use some income to grow our assets!

So here we are. In a moment, we'll do the balancing act.

Time Out for Savings

But first, another word about savings. In Chapter 4 and elsewhere, we've talked about setting up little savings funds, or "strategic reserves," to take care of income fluctuations, irregular musts, contingencies, and special wants. Grade A Numero Uno performance if you've already done it, are committed to it, or are living by it. But you're not *quite* done— there are two more important forms of savings that shouldn't be left out.

Are You the Retiring Type?

Without belaboring the baby-boom-no-Social-Security-someday issue we've all heard too much about, suffice it to say that dice are rolling (that is, you're gambling your retirement away) if you're not saving money for retirement. There are hundreds of vehicles for doing this, all beyond the scope of this book. The point here is that something needs to be set aside. How much? Again, that's another book, but you should put away something. The advantage is that *most* retirement savings plans are tax deferred, so money stuck in retirement savings can have a tax offset (equal to your incremental tax rate times the amount set aside).

Get Your Assets in Gear

It would be a pity to work your tail off for so many years, only to do your net worth calculation and find out that (retirement aside) you're worth no more now than you were when you started your first job! The antidote? Start a growth savings fund. Grow your assets!

Away from Your Hot Little Hands

We'll repeat: this isn't a book about investments. However, recognize that income reserves and must/contingency/want funds are short-term, up-and-down affairs and need to be kept in *liquid* forms of savings—at the bank or at the credit union, for example. "Liquid" means that they can be withdrawn at any time with no penalty. Meanwhile, retirement and growth savings are different. They are long term. They should be untouchable outside of dire emergencies. So mutual funds or other investment vehicles should be set well aside from your normal daily affairs and banking activity—that's what you need.

The Six-Round Knockout

Okay, enough of the preliminaries! Down to business. We started with a budget that looked pretty good. But alas! Musts were uncovered, and nothing was set aside for any form of savings. Deep Bandini if that car stops running today.

Note that in Worksheet 2, we've taken the annual total bill of $1,020 ($900 for car insurance and $120 for renter's) and divided it by 12. The result is $85 placed in a must fund. Every month, $85 will be set aside in this fund, available to pay the bills when they come due.

We told you retirement is important; it comes right after the must fund. How did we pick $100 in Worksheet 3? Nothing scientific, and it probably should be more. But you have to start somewhere. If you get a raise, this should be the first item to grow, because a growth in "musts" caused by a raise is unlikely.

Month of January		
	Item	Balance
GROSS GROSS		$ 3,000
income reserve savings	$ 0	
GROSS		$ 3,000
less payroll taxes, FICA	$ 800	
TAKE HOME		$ 2,200
SAVINGS:		
must fund	$ 85	
rainy day fund	$ 0	
want fund	$ 0	
growth fund	$ 0	
retirement	$ 0	
TOTAL	$ 85	
AVAILABLE		$ 2,115
MUSTS:		
mortgage/rent	$ 500	
property/renters insurance		$120 ONCE/YEAR
property taxes		
property dues or fees		
day care or tuition		
existing car payments	$ 195	
car insurance		$450 TWICE/YEAR
professional dues etc.		
TOTAL MUSTS:	$ 695	
SPENDABLE		$ 1,420
NECESSITIES		
groceries	$ 250	
utilities	$ 120	
phone	$ 50	
gas	$ 50	
medical expenses		
school, lunches, expenses	$ 40	
home maintenance		
dry cleaning	$ 40	
pest control		
cable TV	$ 30	
TOTAL NECESSITIES:	$ 580	
DISCRETIONARY		$ 580
POCKET MONEY	$ 180	
		$ 660
FAMILY DISCRETIONARY		
FAMILY ALLOWANCE	$ 200	$ 460
PERSONAL DISCRETIONARY		
PERSONAL ALLOWANCE	$ 200	
BALANCE		$ 260

Round One—Set up a must fund to cover annual and semi-annual insurance bills.

Month of January			
		Item	Balance
GROSS GROSS			$ 3,000
	income reserve savings	$ 0	
GROSS			$ 3,000
	less payroll taxes, FICA	$ 800	
TAKE HOME			$ 2,200
	SAVINGS:		
	must fund	$ 85	
	rainy day fund	$ 0	
	want fund	$ 0	
	growth fund	$ 0	
	retirement	$ 100	←
	TOTAL	$ 185	
AVAILABLE			$ 2,015
	MUSTS:		
	mortgage/rent	$ 500	
	property/renters insurance		$120 ONCE/YEAR
	property taxes		
	property dues or fees		
	day care or tuition		
	existing car payments	$ 195	
	car insurance		$450 TWICE/YEAR
	professional dues etc		
	TOTAL MUSTS:	$ 695	
SPENDABLE			$ 1,320
	NECESSITIES		
	groceries	$ 250	
	utilities	$ 120	
	phone	$ 50	
	gas	$ 50	
	medical expenses		
	school, lunches, expenses	$ 40	
	home maintenance		
	dry cleaning	$ 40	
	pest control		
	cable TV	$ 30	
	TOTAL NECESSITIES:	$ 580	
DISCRETIONARY			$ 740
POCKET MONEY		$ 180	
			$ 560
FAMILY DISCRETIONARY			
	FAMILY ALLOWANCE	$ 200	$ 360
PERSONAL DISCRETIONARY			
	PERSONAL ALLOWANCE	$ 200	
BALANCE			$ 160

Round Two—Add retirement savings.

Month of January	Item	Balance
GROSS GROSS		$ 3,000
income reserve savings	$ 0	
GROSS		$ 3,000
less payroll taxes, FICA	$ 800	
TAKE HOME		$ 2,200
SAVINGS:		
must fund	$ 85	
rainy day fund	$ 100	
want fund	$ 0	
growth fund	$ 0	
retirement	$ 100	
TOTAL	$ 285	
AVAILABLE		$ 1,915
MUSTS:		
mortgage/rent	$ 500	
property/renters insurance		$120 ONCE/YEAR
property taxes		
property dues or fees		
day care or tuition		
existing car payments	$ 195	
car insurance		$450 TWICE/YEAR
professional dues etc		
TOTAL MUSTS:	$ 695	
SPENDABLE		$ 1,220
NECESSITIES		
groceries	$ 250	
utilities	$ 120	
phone	$ 50	
gas	$ 50	
medical expenses		
school, lunches, expenses	$ 40	
home maintenance		
dry cleaning	$ 40	
pest control		
cable TV	$ 30	
TOTAL NECESSITIES:	$ 580	
DISCRETIONARY		$ 640
POCKET MONEY	$ 180	
		$ 460
FAMILY DISCRETIONARY		
FAMILY ALLOWANCE	$ 200	$ 260
PERSONAL DISCRETIONARY		
PERSONAL ALLOWANCE	$ 200	
BALANCE		$ 60

Round Three—Set up rainy day fund.

A rainy day fund? What for? We don't know—but something will break. Your car, your tooth, your cat. Add a hundred bucks in Worksheet 4. Where are we? Still $60 ahead! What have we missed?

Everybody has a list of "wants," things big enough to be "budget bombs" if left otherwise unattended. So let's get them in. We've added a few: $500 toward a $1,000 refrigerator (more on the "50-50 rule" in Chapter 8), $200 for a new camera, $200 for a new winter coat, and $300 for a gift fund. The total is $1,200 for the year. January's budget allocation? A hundred dollars to the want fund in Worksheet 5.

Done? Checking the balance ... uh-oh, negatory! Forty bucks in the hole. There's work left to do.

Gotta come up with forty bucks somewhere. You knew this was going to happen: those happy allowances you set aside to do whatever you and your family wanted may have been too generous. Not to fret—you'll lose a little here, but gain by getting what's on your wants list. Take twenty bucks out of the family allowance and twenty from your PAL. The good news is, your budget is balanced in Worksheet 6, and you still have 90 percent of each allowance left!

This last category's completely up to you (Okay, so they *all* are). We think it's a good idea to allocate some portion of your income to asset growth, so we reallocated another $30 from your PAL. We'll also ask you to iron five of your own shirts a month, saving $10 from the dry-cleaning bill (under necessities; see Worksheet 7). You can do it however you want—chicken instead of beef, unsweetened cereal instead of Alpha Bits, generic toilet paper. All up to you; it's your budget!

You're done!

Month of January		Item		Balance	
GROSS GROSS				$	3,000
	income reserve savings	$	0		
GROSS				$	3,000
	less payroll taxes, FICA	$	800		
TAKE HOME				$	2,200
	SAVINGS:				
	must fund	$	85		
	rainy day fund	$	100		
	want fund	$	100		←
	growth fund	$	0		
	retirement	$	100		
	TOTAL	$	385		
AVAILABLE				$	1,815
	MUSTS:				
	mortgage/rent	$	500		
	property/renters insurance			$120 ONCE/YEAR	
	property taxes				
	property dues or fees				
	day care or tuition				
	existing car payments	$	195		
	car insurance			$450 TWICE/YEAR	
	professional dues etc				
	TOTAL MUSTS:	$	695		
SPENDABLE				$	1,120
	NECESSITIES				
	groceries	$	250		
	utilities	$	120		
	phone	$	50		
	gas	$	50		
	medical expenses				
	school, lunches, expenses	$	40		
	home maintenance				
	dry cleaning	$	40		
	pest control				
	cable TV	$	30		
	TOTAL NECESSITIES:	$	580		
DISCRETIONARY				$	540
POCKET MONEY		$	180		
				$	360
FAMILY DISCRETIONARY					
	FAMILY ALLOWANCE	$	200	$	160
PERSONAL DISCRETIONARY					
	PERSONAL ALLOWANCE	$	200		
BALANCE				$	(40)

Round Four—Budget the big wants. Set aside a want fund for a new refrigerator (50 percent), a new camera ($200), a new coat ($200), and a gift fund ($300).

Month of January				
		Item		Balance
GROSS GROSS			$	3,000
	income reserve savings	$ 0		
GROSS			$	3,000
	less payroll taxes, FICA	$ 800		
TAKE HOME			$	2,200
	SAVINGS:			
	must fund	$ 85		
	rainy day fund	$ 100		
	want fund	$ 100		
	growth fund	$ 0		
	retirement	$ 100		
	TOTAL	$ 385		
AVAILABLE			$	1,815
	MUSTS:			
	mortgage/rent	$ 500		
	property/renters insurance			$120 ONCE/YEAR
	property taxes			
	property dues or fees			
	day care or tuition			
	existing car payments	$ 195		
	car insurance			$450 TWICE/YEAR
	professional dues etc			
	TOTAL MUSTS:	$ 695		
SPENDABLE			$	1,120
	NECESSITIES			
	groceries	$ 250		
	utilities	$ 120		
	phone	$ 50		
	gas	$ 50		
	medical expenses			
	school, lunches, expenses	$ 40		
	home maintenance			
	dry cleaning	$ 40		
	pest control			
	cable TV	$ 30		
	TOTAL NECESSITIES:	$ 580		
DISCRETIONARY			$	540
	POCKET MONEY	$ 180		
			$	360
FAMILY DISCRETIONARY				
	FAMILY ALLOWANCE	$ 180	$	180
PERSONAL DISCRETIONARY				
	PERSONAL ALLOWANCE	$ 180		
BALANCE				$0

*Round Five—Climbing out. Over budget $40. Cut Personal
Allowance and Family Allowance $20 each to make room for
"want."*

Month of January		Item		Balance	
GROSS GROSS				$	3,000
	income reserve savings	$	0		
GROSS				$	3,000
	less payroll taxes, FICA	$	800		
TAKE HOME				$	2,200
	SAVINGS:				
	must fund	$	85		
	rainy day fund	$	100		
	want fund	$	100		
	growth fund	$	40		
	retirement	$	100		
	TOTAL	$	425		
AVAILABLE				$	1,775
	MUSTS:				
	mortgage/rent	$	500		
	property/renters insurance				$120 ONCE/YEAR
	property taxes				
	property dues or fees				
	day care or tuition				
	existing car payments	$	195		
	car insurance				$450 TWICE/YEAR
	professional dues etc				
	TOTAL MUSTS:	$	695		
SPENDABLE				$	1,080
	NECESSITIES				
	groceries	$	250		
	utilities	$	120		
	phone	$	50		
	gas	$	50		
	medical expenses				
	school, lunches, expenses	$	40		
	home maintenance				
	dry cleaning	$	30		←
	pest control				
	cable TV	$	30		
	TOTAL NECESSITIES:	$	570		
DISCRETIONARY				$	510
POCKET MONEY		$	180		
				$	330
FAMILY DISCRETIONARY					
	FAMILY ALLOWANCE	$	180	$	150
PERSONAL DISCRETIONARY					
	PERSONAL ALLOWANCE	$	150		←
BALANCE				$0	

*Round Six—The last punch: Assets. Create room for Growth
Savings ($10 from ironing a few of your own shirts, $30
more from PAL).*

It's Over—Now What?

Now that your budget is finished, it's tempting to set it aside and head out for a nice dinner and evening's entertainment (if covered in your budget). Very nice, but first ....

- Get agreement from everyone in your household.

- Get agreement from *yourself*. You *will not* spend more than $150 a month on personal allowance items, and you *will not* go to the ATM for more than $40 per week, and you *will not* try to sneak in a few "cash over" dollars at the grocery. Remember, the only person you cheat is you!

- Keep totals. If you can do it in your head, great; if not, find another way. This goes for everyone in the household who handles family money. Set up a method and stick to it.

Keep on Readin'

Whew, a family budget at last! Thinking of maybe putting this book back on your nightstand now that you know how to construct a budget? We wouldn't recommend doing that just yet.

Yes, you have a budget now, one that you believe will work for you and your family and put you on the path to financial health and well-being. But what about the big and little pitfalls along the way? What about when *life* happens?

Read on and see what valuable knowledge you can glean from the next few chapters. Learn how to deal with the credit-card bugaboos, plan (and execute) the big purchases, and handle special budget situations, such as being newlyweds or having kids in college.

The Least You Need to Know

- Don't get hung up on finding the best way (ledger paper, computer spreadsheet, stone tablet) to record your budget; accuracy and the ability to carry it out are what count.

- Always make sure your estimates are on track and you don't get stuck with an unexpected tax bill.

- Money left over at the end of your monthly budget should be promptly socked away in savings, not squandered.

- A negative number at the end of the monthly budget should send you back to rework the numbers until it at least comes out even.

Chapter 7

Using Credit When Credit Is Due

In This Chapter

- Using credit wisely
- When *not* to use credit
- Paying your monthly bills
- How many cards do you really need?

In many areas in our lives, we are self-assured and confident of our ability to do a good job. "Sure, I can do that!" is our rallying cry. But when it comes to dealing effectively with our credit cards, some of that bravado falls away. You are not alone by any means; most of us secretly feel that we are in way, way over our heads. So what to do? Put that "can do" attitude to work and learn how to deal with it.

Credit: When to Use It (and When to Run Like Hell)

Credit. The very word would get your grandparents to shaking their heads, frowning, and muttering, "Why, in my day, if we didn't have the money, we just waited! Who ever heard of paying after you buy?" From an early age, most of us get the feeling that credit is, deep down, kind of a sinful thing.

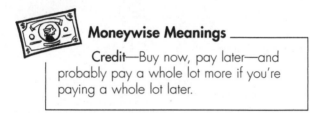

Moneywise Meanings

Credit—Buy now, pay later—and probably pay a whole lot more if you're paying a whole lot later.

But is credit really such a bad thing? Are we, the authors of a book about living on a budget, actually going to give you the thumbs-up about using credit cards? Almost ....

Credit isn't such a bad thing in and of itself, really. It can come in handy and makes great sense in many situations. Let's take a look at some of the times that credit is a fine idea:

- **Business expenses.** When did you take Mr. Biggest Account out to lunch, anyway? Surely the receipt is carefully filed away. Keeping track of assorted business expenses is much easier if they all go on one dedicated credit card.

- **Online commerce.** Of course you need a credit card to shop online. What are you going to do—send Amazon.com a check in the mail? Not. You are going to type in your little numbers and hope like heck that no one out there in cyberspace is watching.

- **Instant accountability.** Remember from the previous chapter how you're going to stick to a monthly personal and family allowance from now on? Does that mean you have to put your credit cards away? It depends on how much willpower you have. If you do continue using cards, you should keep a mental (or written) tab on how much of your allowance you've spent. And what better way to do that than by phoning your credit card's 800 number to see how much you've spent so far this month?

- **Unexpected bargains.** So you've been saving up anyway to buy those new speakers, when suddenly there's a warehouse sale at the stereo store. Your dream speakers are now $200 less! Go ahead. Use your credit card to take advantage of a bargain price on something you were carefully planning to buy anyway, but use the money you've been saving up to pay the credit-card bill when it comes in. What if you have to carry a bit of a balance for a month or two? Make sure the money you have saved by buying it on sale now vastly outweighs the interest you have to pay on the balance.

- **Emergency! Emergency!** If the car breaks down in Death Valley and you don't seem to have much cash (and no one is the least bit interested in taking your out-of-state personal check), of course you're going to use your credit card. Just make sure you have a solid handle on what constitutes an actual emergency—a sunny day and 12 inches of fresh powder on the slopes does not count!

When You Should Run Like Hell

So we've covered the situations in which using a credit card ain't such a bad idea after all. So when is it a budget-busting, send-you-to-the-poorhouse idea to use those pieces of plastic? How about when …

- You are dazzled by the sight of an extremely expensive item that you *know* you can't afford—a gold Rolex watch, a bottle of 25-year-old single-malt scotch, a Channel suit. If you know you can't afford to buy it, then you also can't afford to charge it and pay for it over the next few years.

- Your life seemed full and you were content, at least up until a few minutes ago when you saw an infomercial for [fill in the blank]. A wild impulse has seized you; it wasn't something you knew you needed even five minutes ago. But the commercial or advertisement is sooo compelling that you must have it and you must have it now. Put down that phone! If your life was happy before this impulse seized you, it will still be happy if you completely ignore this sudden desire. And speaking of desire, pitch out those mail-order catalogs, too.

● Your shopping cart is loaded with delicious-looking perishables and all the necessities you need to get through the week—dishwashing liquid, toilet paper, a few magazines, some frozen peas. Pay for your groceries with a credit card? Fine idea, if you pay your bill in full every single month without fail. But if you routinely run a balance, are you *nuts*? Charging something that lasts only as long as the time it takes you to eat it? Paying over months and years for something you ate? Listen carefully—not a good idea!

● The candlelight is enchanting, the music is seductive, the food smells so good ... and you plan to pay for this romantic dinner with your plastic buddy. You pull that credit card out for almost every lunch and breakfast you eat out, too. Just as with groceries, if you pay off your bill in full every single month, this is fine. But if you're digging yourself into debt over meals you ate long ago—arrrgh!

● Think about it—you stop by the neighborhood bar for a quick round after work with some friends and stay for only an hour. However, it could take you months to pay off that part of your credit-card bill. Think twice.

Budget Bombs

Eating out and using a charge card to pay for lunch was Jennifer's big bugaboo a few years back. And then letting the balance build up a tiny bit, and then vowing to pay it all off and then ... well, none of us is perfect. Those lunches out with co-workers ended up costing quite a bundle. Not paying off your monthly balance can create lifelong credit headaches, so try to stay as current as you can.

Merely a Method

Why are we being so mean about your credit card? It isn't any of our business, of course, but we want you to understand how to use it in the wisest, most budget-minded way possible—in a way that won't hold you back from achieving your dreams.

Paying by credit card is using money, just like paying with cash or a personal check. Remember how we left it off the monthly expense list? Despite credit-card bills coming monthly, they are not monthly expenses. So although you don't get to include a monthly $250 credit-card payment on the list of things you've budgeted for, you may well have budgeted for $50 worth of books and magazines, $100 for clothing, $75 for gasoline, and $25 for gifts. Go ahead and pay for those things with a credit card, but be careful not to exceed the budget limits you've set for yourself. Come the end of the month, you *can* pay the bill off in full.

Pay It Off, Pay It Off!

Remember, don't use credit to pay for things that don't last. Of course the romantic dinner was swell, but doesn't the thought that you will be paying for it over the next few months leave a bitter taste in your mouth?

When looking at the "balance due" portion of your credit-card statement, it's all too easy to focus on how *much* you owe, instead of *why* you owe it. Pull out a few old statements and look closely at those charges, just to remind yourself what you're paying for now. Was *that* in your budget?

A Return to the Classroom

Pay attention to what we're saying here. If you're running a balance on your credit cards and are not building up your savings at an equal rate, *you are literally consuming more than you produce!* Do we sound like scolds? Cranky economics professors standing in the front of the room lecturing you about balanced budgets? We really don't mean to scold you, of course. That's not why you bought this book. But we do feel duty-bound to point out this ugly fact.

A recent story on National Public Radio focused on how Americans are learning that *the less they consume, the less they will have to work*. So remember that the next time you are eyeing a cashmere sweater in a mail-order catalog. If you don't buy it, you won't have to work to pay for it. Cool. Of course, Ben Franklin knew this when he said "a penny saved is a penny earned," but Americans seem to have forgotten his wisdom.

Verrry Interrresting

"Laugh-In" jokes aside, the whole concept of paying interest is, in fact, very interesting—interesting from an intellectual standpoint, but distressing from a financial standpoint. To folks who have vowed to live on a budget, it can be downright disastrous!

The amount of interest you will pay on any outstanding loan or balance depends on three factors:

- Interest rate
- Duration of the loan
- Size of the payment

The lower the rate (measured by the *APR*), the shorter the duration, and the larger the payment, the less interest will be paid. Conversely, a loan or balance open for a long period of time at a high interest rate, only serviced by minimum payment, becomes very expensive.

Does this second scenario describe your credit card? You bet. Credit-card interest rates are usually the highest around, with an APR often in excess of 20 percent in an era where money-losing companies and third-world nations can borrow at less than 10 percent. You *knew* that. Bet you didn't know that by making those "minimum amount due" payments gently suggested by your credit-card company, you were signing up to pay off your balance in 10, sometimes 15 *years*. At 20-plus percent, 10 to 15 years can *really* seem like long time!

There is no better way to explain than to illustrate by example.

Moneywise Meanings

APR—Annual percentage rate. The APR is the total amount of interest you would pay on a loan if you owed money for one year, expressed as a percentage of the amount originally borrowed.

Suppose you owe $1,000. We'll examine two popular credit-card interest rates—21.5 percent, a "normal" rate, and 9.9 percent, offered as a "good deal" by some companies. (It isn't a very good deal, but as we'll see it's a whole lot better than 21.5 percent.) In the following table, we'll examine how much interest you will pay at the two different interest rates. You'll see the high-damage case where you pay just the minimum amount due of $20 per month. Then, we'll see how much less damage is done when you "stretch" to pay more than the minimum. It is very clear, and yes, verry interresting ....

Payment		21.5% Interest	9.9% Interest
$20	Time to pay	10 yrs	5 yrs
	Total interest	$1,547	$294
$50	Time to pay	2 yrs	1 yr 10 mos
	Total interest	$248	$85
$100	Time to pay	11 mos	10.5 mos
	Total interest	$111	$48

You can draw your own conclusions.

How Those Credit Guys Make Their Money

Are interest charges the only way banks make money on the zillions of credit cards they have issued? Oh no, far from it. Another aspect of responsible credit card handling is making sure these folks don't get one dime more of your money than you owe them. As the world of credit has become more competitive, companies have been busy dreaming up more ways to profit from their cardholders, to wit …

- **Steeper late charges.** Yes, you thought you paid your bill on time, but did that envelope arrive at its destination on or before the actual due date? Because if it didn't, look for a late charge of $25 or more to be added to your next bill. Think about it—if you sent in a payment of $250, only $225 was actually applied to your balance. The card issuer pocketed a full 10 percent of the money you thought you were paying your bill with. Sure, most of us delay sending in the check until the last minute, but this ought to make you rethink that strategy.

- **Annual fees.** Most credit cards do have a yearly membership fee attached to them. It could be only $25 or $40 dollars, or it could be in excess of $100 for some of the pricey American Express, platinum, or gold cards. Since the fee just shows up on the bill one day, it's all too easy to forget about it. Check your cardholder agreement periodically to make sure you know just how much that card is costing you. Carry more than one card? Then you are probably paying more than one annual fee. It does add up.

- **Cash advances.** This seems like such a great idea. You find yourself a little strapped toward the end of the month, so you stop by the ATM machine and take a cash advance on your credit card. Be warned (strongly warned!) about the true cost of this kind of a loan— you will be paying interest on a cash advance. Even if you pay it off at the end of the month, you will have been charged interest from the moment you put out your hand and received those twenties from the machine. Aside from the interest, you no doubt paid a cash advance fee, too. Interest rates on cash advances can be 24 percent, more than even a loan shark would charge.

Budget Bombs

When is $100 not $100? When it's money you have withdrawn as a cash advance on your credit card. If you take a cash advance of $100, you could owe the credit-card company $1 or $2 *the moment you take the cash out of the ATM!* And then you'll owe more every month.

Not only are all those little fees and interest charges a bad thing, but actually needing a cash advance doesn't bode well for your finances or your budget. It usually means that ...

- You have unbudgeted expenses you can't pay for.
- You have no cash savings to help you with this unexpected expense.
- You are consuming more than you can afford.

If any of these are the case, the situation will only get worse once that cash advance is in your hand.

When Is Credit Not Called Credit?

Marketers are masters of disguise. Time and time again, words like "small" are respun into pleasantries like "quaint" or "cute" when pitching a house for sale. Dull and ordinary become "timeless." These serve no other purpose than to put you, the potential buyer, at ease about potential shortcomings. Where are we going with this? Guess what? They've done it to credit, too.

Pick up the Sunday paper. How many times do you see "no money down" or "90 days same as cash" or "no payments until year 20xx"? Look at the car ads. See the word "loan" or "credit" or "borrow" or "debt" anywhere? Hardly. Everything's a "lease."

What's going on? Yep, marketing. These are financing gimmicks just like "regular" credit. Sometimes there's a twist, but more often it's just a spin.

We'll talk about these and other financing techniques for large purchases in Chapter 8. But make no mistake, they are credit, plain and simple. Sometimes you come out better than "normal" borrowing with these gimmicks, but only in very carefully managed circumstances. Let the borrower beware!

Ah, leasing a car sounds so much easier than buying a car on a long-term loan—which we all know is credit. But is a lease also a form of credit? Heck, yes!

Do You Really Need More Than One Card?

So now that you've made a solemn vow to get credit-card spending under control and you've grasped the ugly truth about how much it costs you to use your cards, how should you deal with the cards you have? Should each household have only one credit card? Who should be in charge of it?

Doesn't sound like the way we'd want to live, and we can't imagine you'd want to live that way, either. Here's what Peter and Jennifer do—we each have a credit card in our own names, and each one is 100 percent responsible for making decisions about how it should be used. We both know exactly how much free reign our budget allows us, however, when it comes to our differing categories, and we try very hard to stay within those guidelines.

In addition to the two all-purpose cards we carry, we have a joint-account card that is used for household expenses. We use a Discover card for purchases such as light bulbs from Home Depot or a new car seat. That way we can easily track these sorts of expenses separately from other kinds of expenses. It seems to work.

In addition to a general all-purpose credit card, such as Visa or MasterCard, what about all those "accessory cards," the department store cards? If you can't bear to give them up, at least leave them at home. Not long ago Jennifer looked carefully at what she had stuffed in her wallet and discovered at least two cards for big fancy department stores that were thousands of miles away from where she lived! Why should a California girl be wandering around with a Bloomingdale's card in her wallet every day? Better to stick it in a drawer and bring it along next time a business trip to New York is planned. In addition to added temptation, carrying multiple cards could also put you at risk if your wallet is stolen. Sure, you remember that you had your Visa card in there, but what the heck else were you carrying? If you carry so many cards that you forget what you have, thin 'em out now before a thief does it for you.

And gasoline cards? Are they still needed in this day and age? If it works for you, keep 'em. But the case of having all your charges on one card statement where you can quickly see if you are staying within the boundaries of your budget can be a big plus. Also, keep an eye on those extra purchases you make every time you fill up—a soda here, a bag of chips there, and pretty soon you've charged an extra $25 on your gas card that didn't go into your tank.

Credit-Card Insurance

Is your mailbox full of solicitations for credit-card insurance? Do telephone solicitors call you during the dinner hour to tell you how cheap it would be for you to buy credit-card insurance? Tell them to leave you alone, and eat your dinner in peace.

Why? Because by law, credit-card owners are already protected. The rules state that you are liable for only $50 per card once you report the card lost or stolen. (Now you know why every time you make a purchase, the clerk "runs" your card or phones it in. Yeah, they check your limit, but even more to see if that card has been reported lost or stolen. To no one's surprise, the credit-card companies are protecting themselves.)

The catch is this: (1) you must report the card lost or stolen, and (2) $50 times 15 or 20 credit cards can still add up to a lot of money. But it still isn't worth spending $59.95 per card per year, is it?

Better to reduce the number of cards to reduce your exposure and make it easier to track their whereabouts.

Also beware … some debit cards (like many of the new bank multipurpose ATM cards) do not carry the $50 protection. Check it out if you have one.

Can I Live Without a Credit Card or Two?

Is it truly possible to live without credit cards? Is that a financial goal we should all be striving for? We don't think it really makes sense. Remember, credit cards and the concept of credit are not inherently bad; it's all in how you use it.

Keep your credit, but keep it wisely. How you handle your credit cards can affect how you will be able to finance a car or buy a house. If the credit report shows that you are a good credit risk who pays in a timely manner, you can get the lowest car loans available. Some people who have never borrowed money at all might find it difficult to get a loan when they decide to buy a house.

Are You in Trouble Now? Go for the Quick Fix

Although we have been encouraging and sympathetic about how living on a budget doesn't need to cramp your style, allow us to abandon the soft tone for a few paragraphs here. If you are in serious trouble with your credit cards, your lifestyle is about to be *seriously* cramped. There is no way to soften this message. You must *immediately* turn all your financial firepower on this problem. Abandon those plans to build up various and sundry financial reserves and to save for vacations—that will have to wait until you pay off your credit cards! No more shopping, no new winter wardrobe, no lunches or dinners out, no treats for you, until you pay this debt way, way down.

You need to immediately do the following:

- Pay off the card with the highest interest rate first.
- Consider transferring all your credit-card debt onto one card with a low interest rate, and immediately stop using all your old cards. Do not run up the balance *again*!

What you should not do under any circumstances:

- Sign up for more credit cards so you can get cash advances to make other payments.
- Take out a home equity loan to pay off your credit-card bills.
- Take out a debt consolidation loan.

Why not? Because you will imperil your own financial future, you won't learn anything about how to handle credit cards in the future, and you stand a huge risk of ending up even further in debt! You might also lose your home.

According to the Debt Counselors of America, about 80 percent of people who get a debt consolidation loan find themselves in deeper debt and bigger trouble than they were before. Think about it—*you cannot borrow your way out of debt!* The Debt Counselors of America can help you (for free!). Check out their website at www.getoutofdebt.org.

The Least You Need to Know

- Credit is not a bad thing if you learn to use it wisely.
- Never use your credit card to purchase impulse items you cannot afford.
- When charging purchases, stick to the budget categories you have already established.
- Besides charging interest on balances, credit-card companies make money off you in several other ways.
- Go ahead and carry an all-purpose card with you, but leave the department store cards at home.
- Never refinance your home or take out a debt consolidation loan to clear up your credit-card debts.

Chapter 8

Making *Big* Purchases

In This Chapter

- Deciding "needs" versus "wants"
- Ask yourself—can you do without it?
- The fix-it, clean-it, borrow-it alternative
- Bargain often, bargain always

It has been said, "Take care of the necessities, and the luxuries will take care of themselves." We've also been told, "Take care of the pennies, and the dollars will take care of themselves." Wouldn't it be nice if that were all we had to worry about?

So far we've focused on the groceries and gas, not the refrigerator and car they go in. And despite the lovely sentiments expressed in these old-fashioned quotations, we firmly believe you *must* pay attention to the *big purchases*.

There are a lot of choices, and you are 100 percent in control of how much you spend on them. Done right, the impact of big purchases can be minimized and even turned into a positive experience for your personal finances. Done wrong, they can be first-order (nuclear) budget bombs.

Let's take a short walk through the car lots and appliance floors of life, and get some ideas about how to make the big purchases work for you. Why, maybe they can even be fun!

Moneywise Meanings

What is a **"big purchase"**? Good question. In this book, a big purchase is something you buy less often than once every five years, so that stack of CDs for your jazz collection really doesn't count here.

Need Not, Want Not

Think you need something big? The first question to ask yourself (and it seems so obvious) is whether you *really* need it!

It's gratifying to see the fruits of our labor sitting in the driveway or dock, making life in the kitchen or yard easy, making our hobbies happen. We get *control*. We can use it *when* we want, *how* we want, *where* we want. We get *status*.

It's not our goal to deny you these privileges (nor would we want to)! This is America, after all, the land of the free. But wise and disciplined budgeters take steps to guard their financial freedom by asking a few questions and exploring a few alternatives before signing up for that big purchase.

How to Get By Without Buying

Simply buying something is the easy way out—but it's not easy on your finances! It's new, it fits all your needs and then some, and it's a source of pride as well as function. The fly in the ointment: you have to pay for it. Since you bought it new, well, you know what that means—you probably paid top dollar.

If you need to buy, you need to buy. But there's a little checklist to go through first.

Alternative 1: Fix It

Ah, the age-old dilemma. Your eight-year-old car has 100,000 miles on it, and you blew a head gasket. Eight hundred dollars will get you on the road again, but it also gets you thinking. Shouldn't you just go out and buy a new car instead of sinking a bunch of dough into a car that will probably need another major repair in the next few years? Is it really time to buy a new one?

Not necessarily. Even though $800 is a big budget-buster for most of us, it could still be the right choice. If the rest of the car is fairly sound, it *is* the right choice.

Why? Well, for starters, think about this—$800 won't even pay the sales tax on most new car purchases (in states that have sales tax, that is)—not to mention finance charges, registration fees, higher car insurance, and so forth. We'll talk about knowing all the costs later, but the point is that good financial decisions mean weighing alternatives, not just financing the purchase.

There are many other examples—replacing drive belts on the washer or vacuum instead of replacing the washer or vacuum, replacing bad boards in the deck instead of replacing the whole deck, and so forth. The check you write might seem big at the time, but not compared to checks you'll write over a long period of time to finance a big purchase instead of a big repair.

Alternative 2: Clean It

Clean it? What kind of silly advice is that? It's not so silly, really. It has everything to do with what we think of ourselves and how others perceive us. So maybe you think your shabby old car looks like it ought to be replaced, and you'd blush with shame if you thought anyone actually saw you behind the wheel of it. Rather than replace it, can you just spend a bit having it washed, waxed, and detailed? Beats buying a new car, and you'd be surprised how big a difference it makes.

123 By the Numbers

By keeping her old college car fairly neat and clean, Jennifer was always somewhat perversely pleased that on the parking tickets she'd get (so who's perfect?), her seven-year-old Toyota was always described by the meter maid as being the most current model available. Hey, you've got to take whatever joy you can find in a parking ticket!

More than just cars can be given a second wind
through careful cleaning—appliances can be over-
hauled; furniture can be refinished, reupholstered,
or dressed up with a cool blanket or throw; and
clothing can be restyled. Before you toss out an old
and faithful big-ticket item and head to the mall,
consider whether it can be reconditioned and used
for a few more years.

Alternative 3: Rent It or Borrow It

We might have mentioned in an earlier chapter
that Peter really, really wants an expensive piece of
woodworking machinery, a band saw. Alas, we've
never actually gotten around to adding it to our list
of items we're saving for. Does he mope around,
looking longingly at the tool catalogs that arrive in
the mail? Nope, he walks across the street and uses
our neighbor Scott's band saw instead.

Does every American household really need to
own a riding lawn mower, multi-attachment food
processor, or pressure washer? Why not save your
money and rent the equipment you need for a day
or a weekend? Or work out a swap with your neighbors. They might well prefer to borrow some expensive item you own rather than spring for one of
their own. Perhaps your budget-wise ways will begin
to influence everyone around you.

Alternative 4: Barter or Swap for It

Jennifer had a cool suede jacket (she bought it at a
consignment shop, of course) that a friend coveted.

The friend had something that Jennifer coveted, too … a wine shop. So they worked out a deal. The shop owner got to use Jennifer's jacket for a month or two, and Jennifer got a very pricey bottle of French champagne she otherwise would never buy.

What do you already have that you can use to your advantage? Perhaps you can swap or loan it in exchange for another item you crave. Maybe what you have is a skill or talent that can be used to get your heart's desire. Can you help a small business owner with publicity in exchange for a sweetheart deal?

Alternative 5: Do Without It

Doing without it sounds like the toughest one of all. You have the itch. Life would be utopia if you had it. Your friends and family would be impressed, and you would never dally on beautiful weekends wondering what you would do with yourself and your family. What is it? Doesn't matter.

Just think about it—very carefully. Do you really need it? With the money you save, even better rewards may await. If you're really clever, there might be ways to enjoy it anyway, without carrying the full cost burden.

Take, for example, a pleasure boat. In most climates, with the pressures of other family needs and activities, would you use it more than, say, 20 times a year? With storage, maintenance, insurance, taxes, and depreciation on the original purchase, a $10,000 boat would certainly cost $3,000/year. What a nice vacation that would pay for! A two-week driving trip to Florida, a cruise, a short Hawaii trip. And you never have to worry about selling an old boat. Which is better?

Budget Bombs

Thinking about replacing the dishwasher but still making payments to Sears for the old one? Checking out brand-new cars but still far from paying off the one you already own? It's harder to get ahead if you replace items you haven't yet paid for.

Now that you've thought *that* through, and you're still set on the boat, well, okay. You've gotten this far, and we don't want you to throw this book away now. So what are the choices?

First, as we've suggested before, look into rentals or buying used. Obvious. Not so obvious is this: If you have friends, family, or neighbors also interested in boating or who already have boats, they're probably in exactly the same boat (sorry!). Here's a solution: go in together. If your neighbor has a boat, offer to help maintain it. Offer to pay winter storage or half the interest on his loan or insurance. Help with spring cleanup and launch. Run errands, or get parts and supplies. Of course, some kind of clear deal needs to be made, but it's an obvious win-win solution for most. Think about it.

Savvy Saver

Never overlook the *cost of ownership.* When buying (almost) anything, you need to think about *all* the costs. Transaction costs, upkeep, insurance, depreciation (loss of value over time), supplies, and consumables. The budget-bomb bay doors are open.

The same deal could apply to swimming pools, vacation homes and timeshares, large tools, collectible cars, or even smaller things, such as that Cuisinart, camera, or big-screen TV. Be creative, and reward yourself for your creativity! It can be fun.

Necessity Never Made a Good Bargain

Or "Buy in haste, repent in leisure." Whichever old Franklinesque phrase you like to use, it's true. Urge-driven, hasty buying almost never yields as good a result as a carefully thought-out purchase. And they can see you coming! Unless you're one of the world's great poker players, you probably have it written all over your face: EASY SALE! With just a little effort, you can turn a seller's market into a buyer's market. It's cheap(er) and it's fun!

Can You Do Any Better on the Price?

Much of the fun of traveling to exotic places is the opportunity to engage in a distinctly un-American pursuit—haggling at a market. But who says you can't do it in your own language as well? When buying a big-ticket item, always, always, always ask for a discount. If the actual word "discount" embarrasses you, there are other ways to say it:

- "Hmmm ... I'd really planned to spend less. Is this your best price?"

- "Does this go on sale anytime soon?" Don't be surprised if it does, and they offer you a special "pre-sale" price.

- "Gosh, $800. That's an awful lot of money ...." Sigh wistfully, and then *don't say anything more!* The salesperson, dreading the long silence, will probably jump in and offer you a lower price somehow.

Sound sort of nervy? It really does work, even in major department stores. There's so much competition nowadays in almost any retail area that you might find the staff much more willing to bend on price than ever before. Give it a try.

What's Old Is New (to You)

If you decide that you really *do* need new dining-room furniture, why not consider shopping for a used or antique set first? If you plunk down the money for brand-new furniture, it won't retain much of its value should you decide to get rid of it someday. However, if you buy a sturdy antique dining room set, and keep it nicely polished and cared for over the years, you might well be able to sell it for pretty much what you paid for it!

Not sure what's an actual antique or what you should pay? There are dozens of non-antique dining sets and other kinds of large pieces of furniture (some of them low quality) advertised in newspapers every day. People sell them for all kinds of legitimate reasons—moving, marriage, divorce, style change. They are good deals at a fraction of the cost (no sales tax, either), and you can bargain with these vendors.

The same theory can work for classic cars, computers, appliances, tools, some kinds of jewelry, and clothing. We'd suggest that you find an expert to separate good deals from bad, especially for items like computers, when six months can turn a good deal into a bad one. Take a computer-knowledgeable friend to dinner for his or her help. You'll save in the long run.

We're not so enthused about garage sales, flea markets, auctions, and so forth. If you have a very specific goal in mind, such as items for a new baby, well, okay. Not long ago, Jennifer was pleased to find a lightly used Combi stroller at a garage sale for $20. Seems like a lot to pay for something at a garage sale, but she knew that a brand-new Combi stroller would cost upward of $200! Such a deal.

If you don't go out looking for a specific item, however, you run the risk of buying stuff you don't need in the ironic interest of "bargains." And then what happens? These things sit around unused and collecting dust until the next time *you* have a garage sale. Auctions and garage sales are a fun and cheap form of entertainment (compared to an overnight gambling junket), but not a recommended way to achieve your budget goals.

123 By the Numbers

A *Wall Street Journal* article on living beneath your means quoted a financial planner, Eleanor Blayney, who suggested that consumers "start thinking of sales discounts as equivalent to percentage returns on your money." So the greater the savings, the greater the return on your investment in that item. A penny saved really is a penny earned!

No Money Down

You open the Sunday paper, and there's the ad: "No money down, no payments, and no interest 'til next January!" Sounds good? Well, maybe. Sure, why pay now when you can pay later? No interest? Sounds good, too. What's the catch? Simply, if you don't pay *in full* by January, you're charged full interest (usually high credit-card rates) all the way back to when you bought it. Cumulative. Not starting from then, starting from *now*! Sooo … it's an okay idea, *as long as you know you can pay it all by January!*

Savvy Saver

No-money-down is a good way to handle contingencies if your contingency fund is "lean." The no-interest period spreads the burden across several months, making up for what you weren't able to accomplish with your contingency fund. But don't buy it unless you do need it, and you *must* pay it off before it comes due to avoid all that interest!

Outside the Showroom

The classic American way to buy big things is simply to trot down to the local showroom or store, ask a few questions, work out a deal and financing, get some instructions about how to use it, buy a few accessories, and go out the door! A little help from the salesperson, some company literature, "word of mouth" advice, and your own common sense.

Like everything else, this is changing. In the '60s, we started getting more consumer information to guide us through purchases. Sources like *Consumer Reports*, or Ralph Nader and his friends, were suddenly releasing information that could help you make a wise choice, but you still had to buy the darn thing from a dealer or store.

Savvy Saver _____

Consumer Reports magazine is chock-full of information that will help you make wise purchases. While the emphasis is more on rating products for quality rather than price or cost-comparison, the more information you have, the better your ability to choose a product that will last for years. You can check out their website for free at www.consumerreports. org, but to access the ratings online you'll need to subscribe.

Now, in the new millennium, alternatives are showing up everywhere. Not that the showroom is always the wrong place—that's where the selection is, that's where the salesperson is, the reputation, the service after the sale (make sure you ask about service). But there are other ways: online purchases, buying services, and buying "slightly" used merchandise at substantial bargains.

A Fingerprint or Two, Otherwise New

Rules have gotten tougher about what a manufacturer can call "new." A computer printer that's been sold and removed from the box, with two or three practice pages printed, can no longer be resold as new if it's returned. So what? Well, most manufacturers have more of this returned stuff than they know what to do with. They need to get rid of it. That's where you and your sharp eye for bargains come in.

> **Savvy Saver** _____
>
> Hanging on to old appliances that still work would seem to be the best approach for budgeters, but it isn't always the case. Due to the consumer's increased emphasis on water and energy efficiency, many of the newer models can pay for themselves in the long term through lower utility bills. Front-loading washing machines, for instance, use far less water and consume less power than the traditional models. Devotees even claim that front-loading washing machines actually clean better, too.

Here's where to look:

- **On the retail floor.** Manufacturers motivate retailers to resell items as "open box" (so as not to incur the cost of returns). These open box items come with a full warranty and usually are inspected. Look for deals like this at Home Depot, Sears, and Circuit City.

- **At manufacturers' and company outlet stores.** Not every outlet store is really worth it. Over the years they have slipped into the realm of ordinary shopping with just a few real finds. But the finds can be had if you look hard enough. Skip the bigger retail clothing brand names and look closely at smaller chains like Restoration Hardware. We've found very good furniture prices on pieces that were returned slightly used by customers and then sent out to the outlet store in Vacaville, California.

In Good Company

A special opportunity exists to buy cars in most parts of the country—buying used fleet cars from large U.S. companies or rental car firms. Because of the gigantic volumes purchased, these companies get good deals from the manufacturers and favorable tax benefits for selling after a scant year or so. You can buy these cars sometimes direct from companies, sometimes from dealers who buy them as "special purchase" items. What you get is an almost new car (12,000–15,000 miles) in great condition, professionally maintained, with a valid remaining warranty—at two thirds the price! These deals are definitely worth looking at the next time you think about buying a new car.

America's Online

Like you, we spend a lot of time online, much of it focused on scoping out a bargain here and there (particularly kids' stuff!). For the most part, we think this is a good way to buy, particularly things you already know about. The prices are generally lower because you avoid paying for stores and salesfolk. Watch out for surprises in the form of shipping charges, however.

> **Savvy Saver**
>
> Online shopping for cars, too? But of course! At www.autoweb.com, you select a vehicle, Autoweb sends you a list of nearby dealers and prices, and then, if you want, a dealer calls you. No more kicking tires. You might also check out www.autobytel.com.

Buyer Beware

Anybody who's bought anything big has had this experience. You make your selection, tell the salesperson, fill out the purchase order, and have the sale rung up. Simultaneously, relief and concern descend upon you. Relief that the decision has been made, and concern about how it affects your future finances. This is mostly a good thing, except for one little problem.

While your mind is focused on this agony and ecstasy, your salesperson is quietly, or not so quietly, adding some items and "ideas" to your bill. Floor mats, pin stripes, polyglycoat—all usually well over $100. No big deal. You just spent 25 grand, right? On the contrary.

The true test of whether it's a good idea: step back and ask yourself if you would spend $160 on those floor mats if you were walking around a store and spotted them any other day. Chances are the answer is no. It's no different on big-purchase day. A hundred and sixty bucks is a hundred and sixty bucks, even with the promise to bury it in your car payment.

Extended Poverty

What about those extended warranties? Generally speaking, they're another avoidable add-on. In many cases, this is where dealers or retailers make most of their profit! Is that warning enough? The truth about these warranties is that they are just expensive, and sometimes tricky, insurance.

Consider the $1,800 warranty they want to sell you for your $18,000 car. Five years, 75,000 miles, "bumper to bumper." Sounds like everything's covered forever, doesn't it? Think again. First of all, your car is probably covered by the normal warranty for 36,000 miles or three years, so the window of protection is only about two years.

Moreover—and here's the point—for $1,800 you could pay for a good-sized repair job straight up— *if* it's ever necessary. In most cases, it's better to take the chance that your car *won't* need repairs. (If the likelihood of major repair really *is* high, maybe you should buy a different car.) Furthermore, often you'll find in the fine print that these extended warranties don't cover everything anyway. Just try to get those interior squeaks fixed at 60,000 miles ....

We feel much the same about extended warranties for lower-cost products. A $60 warranty for a $500 dishwasher doesn't make sense. You have the normal warranty, and a house-call repair costs little more than that.

However, there may be times to purchase the warranty. True confession—we did buy a $65 two-year warranty for a $300 iPod, but only because it was going to be used by a 10-year-old! We think that was a valid investment.

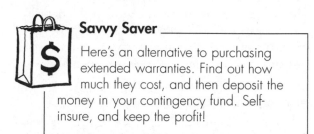

Savvy Saver

Here's an alternative to purchasing extended warranties. Find out how much they cost, and then deposit the money in your contingency fund. Self-insure, and keep the profit!

Rebates and Other Gimmicks

When you shop (or just read the newspaper) you'll find all sorts of ways to pretend you're not spending as much as you are. Rebates, no-money-down, trade-ins, special financing plans. We won't go into them all here. The best advice is to sit down with a cool head and a calculator (or someone else who's good at the numbers) and figure it out. Look at the straight-up cost, without gimmicks, and compare it to the "net" purchase cost with the gimmick. Include all finance charges and fees.

Leasing It Up

One of the great budget pitfalls is to lease, rather than buy, a car. Leasing came to the consumer world from the business world. A lease is nothing more than a commitment to pay a fixed monthly payment for a fixed time, with the asset reverting back to the owner at the end of that time, subject to a (usually) long list of conditions. So what? Well, now lease offers show up everywhere. Why? The word *lease* sounds better than *credit*, and it's something that businesses do all the time, so it must be a good thing, right?

In the consumer world, a lease in lieu of purchase (we're talking cars here, not apartments and so forth) is nothing more than a glorified (and usually expensive) way to finance. You pay a usually small (part of the attraction) upfront fee, and then a fixed monthly payment for, say, 36 months. At the end of the lease, you usually have two choices: (1) Turn the keys back in and walk away, or (2) buy the car at a price ("residual value") determined at the time of initial leasing. And always, in the fine print, there could be extra rental-car-type mileage charges if you drive, say, over 12,000 miles a year.

There's some good news, however: "In" cost (down payments) is low, payments are roughly equal to a loan, credit requirements are usually less, and sales tax that you would pay upfront in a purchase is spread throughout the lease.

But the bad news is that you own—and pay for— the full cost of the car during the most expensive years of ownership. You pay finance charges (indeed) and the difference between purchase price and residual, which reflects the heaviest depreciation years. Then, if you drive more than 12,000 miles, you pay even more. Finally, at the end of three years, you have nothing, and the dealer is waiting to start all over again with you. The problem is that you never reach the low-cost part of the car ownership cycle, where depreciation and insurance are low. If you don't believe us, let's look at some numbers. Just for kicks, let's do the numbers on leasing a small SUV. Here is the offer: Buy for $21,988, or lease for $298 (plus tax) for 42 months. The residual value is $12,552. You need $3,295 down to start. Mileage over 12,000 a year is billed at 15 cents per mile. Auto loans go at 8.5 percent per year. Which is best? (Sorry if this example brings back unkind memories of those eighth-grade algebra word problems.)

Purchase:

Put $3,295 down and finance $18,693.

The minivan is worth $12,522 at the end of 3 years (we'll use their assumption).

At 8.5 percent per year for 42 months, your monthly payment is $516. Sounds like a lot, but most of that is principal payment. You'll spend $2,983 in interest over the 42 months.

Total cost:

$21,988–12,522 = $9,466 depreciation, or lost value, plus $2,983 interest, equals $12,449 total cost.

And you have something worth $12,522 at the end.

Lease:

Put $3,295 down. You don't get it back!

Pay $298 per month × 42 months, or $12,516 total in lease payments.

Total cost:

Your down payment of $3,295 plus lease payments totaling $12,516 equals $15,811.

And you have *nothing* at the end, and you need wheels!

The lease is almost $3,000 more expensive before we consider that you have nothing at the end. You lost your down payment and have to come up with another. Drove an extra 5,000 miles? Add another 750 bucks. And cars aren't getting any cheaper. The car you buy or lease in 42 months will be even more expensive, and since it's new, you will pay more insurance. But you can't afford a $516 payment? Yes, we hear you. But if you were to save about $8,000 more before making this purchase, you would have the same monthly payment as for the leased car, but have all the benefits of ownership and none of the disadvantages of the lease.

The Fifty-Fifty Strategy

We heartily endorse the 50-50 method of making big purchases—using 50 percent savings and financing the other 50 percent. That way your refrigerator/snow blower/camera won't be a 100 percent credit drain, but you won't have to wait until you've saved up the entire purchase price. You still have to wait until you've saved up half the purchase price, though. So you still have months to consider whether you truly need this big-ticket item, whether you have truly found the best deal, or whether this is something you can live without.

The Least You Need to Know

- Think before you replace something you already own. Can you clean it, fix it, rent or borrow it, or do without it altogether?

- Watch out for gimmicks like rebates, leases, unnecessary add-ons, and extended warranties.

- Online shopping and price comparison let you escape the high-pressure tactics of a salesperson who works on commission.

- One great strategy to handle big purchases is to pay 50 percent in cash and finance the other 50 percent.

Special Budget Scenarios

In This Chapter

- Husbands, wives, and money
- Getting off to a good newlywed start
- Dealing with children's money demands
- Saving for college

Living happily on a budget seems so clear-cut. Your life from here on will be one delightful stroll in the budgeting park, at least until you step in something unexpected. Situations do change, and life and finances change right along with them. What kinds of special budget scenarios can arise? Can you imagine anything from this list happening any time soon?

- Once you were single, but now you're not.
- Once your toddler was happy with whatever came his way, but now he has begun to ask for the expensive toys he sees in television commercials.
- Once you had a high school senior at home, but now you have a college freshman.

- Once your child didn't care about shopping, but now threatens your carefully balanced budget with trips to the mall.

Let's take a closer look at these special situations and see how they can best be incorporated into your new dedication to sticking to a budget.

Comin' from the Chapel

Ah, those first few weeks, months, and years as a newlywed. The perfect time to enjoy the bliss of romantic love. What couple would shatter the calm by fighting about something as pedestrian as money? The answer is—most newlywed couples.

Face it, most fights between most couples are about money. Sometimes it's an obvious fight about money ("You paid how much for that??"), and sometimes the money demon is just lying there below the surface of the argument ("I work hard all day, and never have anything to show for it!"). This doesn't mean you made a mistake and married the wrong person (we hope); it just means you're both completely normal.

One of the great things about the first part of a marriage is that it gives you an incredible opportunity to build something together from scratch. Some of the folks reading this book might already have years of money-battle scars. Learning to live happily on a budget will come as a great relief to those weary folks. But you, you lucky newlyweds, you get a once-in-a-lifetime chance to start off together without any money mistakes! By working and planning your budget together, you should be able to avoid many of the money pitfalls. Wedlock should not lead to financial deadlock!

What *Is* Money for, Anyway?

Did you talk about money during your courtship? If you didn't, don't despair. Once again, it just means you're pretty darn normal. Money attitudes might have surfaced in the way you or your fiancé behaved, but few couples actually talk about it directly. Now that you're married, however, you can't put it off any longer! You both need to sit down and discuss your money attitudes.

Choose a pleasant setting, and make a nice occasion of the evening. You should each take a blank sheet of paper and tackle the following questions:

● What is money for?

● What was my family's attitude toward money?

Just two simple questions, but ones that should help you get a handle on how your spouse's mind works when it comes to money. Unless you can come to an agreement about something as basic as "What is money for?", you will have quite a struggle developing a budget and sticking to it.

The Common Goal

After answering the questions, are you surprised to see that you two are rather far apart in your answers? One mate thinks money is for safety and security, while the other mate thinks money is for buying lots of luxurious goodies? Hmmm …. Don't call the divorce lawyer yet; you can work on this together. But you must work on it *together*—you must develop a synchronized attitude toward the role money will play in your life. You must strive toward a common goal.

Remember all the fun goal-setting exercises earlier in the book? Where you got to write down your short-term, medium-term, and long-term financial goals? All that stuff about wanting to buy a new set of skis in the next year, make a down payment on a house in the next five years, and own a donut franchise in the next 12 years? For newlyweds, the goal-making part of putting together a budget is crucial. Please go back and review those pages, particularly the part about not laughing at your spouse's list of goals. Work on creating goals that can support your hearts, your dreams, and your efforts.

Wedding-Bell Blues

One immediate common goal you can work toward is paying off the wedding and the honeymoon! Sure, some lucky folks get a free ride from their parents, but many more of us have to foot the wedding bill ourselves. So why not make that your first financial goal—to clear up any debt you acquired during the ceremony or (more likely) afterward on the beach with a drink in your hand.

Savvy Saver

Doing the grocery shopping together can be a great way for couples to learn about their spouse's money habits and philosophy. It can also help you two develop your own special philosophy, one that doesn't come courtesy of your family's attitudes toward money and spending. Don't make the grocery store a weekly battleground. Don't poke fun at the spouse who brings coupons along. Use this time to talk more about how you both believe your money should be spent.

Skeletons in the Closet

Now that you're married, was there a little something you've been meaning to share with your new spouse? The small matter of a past-due loan, a five-digit credit-card bill, or an old student loan? Do you owe members of your own family a bunch of money? Whatever kind of financial secret you kept to yourself (or whatever you suspect your spouse might be reluctant to share with you), out with it! Better to drag all the bad news into the light and start dealing with it than to go on any longer under the burden of guilt you've been carrying alone.

Will your new spouse be angry? Probably, and he or she probably has a right to be. Married people share a lot, and a credit rating is one of the things you're now sharing! If your little secret is endangering your spouse's credit status, the longer it goes on, the greater the chance that serious damage will be done. Put aside your fear and confess today.

Setting up a New Household

Another really swell thing about getting married is the gifts! Box after box from Crate and Barrel, Macy's, and even Home Depot (now that they've added a wedding registry). Every box filled with some shiny item for your new household. Did you get enough toasters? Bread machines? Pots and pans? Some lucky couples rake in enough loot that they don't have to make a trip to the store to fill out the rest of their household needs. But others might find themselves a bit short of the necessities.

Warning, warning! Setting up a new household is an expensive proposition. Is it right to start your marriage off with a huge debt to the housewares department of a major department store? No. Before you park your car at the mall and start to stock up on new stuff, take the time to review the chapter in this book on credit, as well as the chapter on big purchases.

The same goes for filling your new place with fancy furniture. Before you buy that swanky suede sofa, think about all the other things you two could use that money for, and then call your mom and ask if you can have the old plaid couch from the den.

Newlyweds who struggle together can look back later and giggle at how poor they were. It will give you something to tell your kids (more about them and money coming up soon!).

Off to a Great Start

Newlyweds who embrace the need to budget carefully from the get-go are starting off on a great adventure together. By creating common financial goals together, by developing a shared sense of the proper role of money in their lives, and by designing and staying with a workable budget, these lucky folks will forge a strong bond. Working together to achieve financial goals—and actually achieving them—can help couples build strong marriages that withstand the test of time.

123 By the Numbers

Attorney and financial counselor William Devine, author of the book *Women, Men, and Money*, cautions that in a marriage, "Regardless of your tax bracket, money can produce anxiety." He adds that no matter what your income is, "a fight with your partner over how to invest your savings is a fight with your partner."

So once your new marriage is headed in the right financial direction, what other kinds of unforeseen events might arise? Well, children, for one.

Teach Your Children Well

If you and your new spouse commit to living on a budget, and any little ones who arrive grow up in a household where the money philosophy is clear, you stand a good chance of raising children with a healthy attitude toward money. But if you're coming to the budget table for the first time, will your kids fall in line right behind you? Guess again. If you have a household of kids who are accustomed to hitting you up for a spare $20 on a regular basis, they will not be pleased about this new family budget business. Not pleased at all. It's hard to change ingrained habits, but it can be done.

If your children are younger and have not yet developed a sense of entitlement, great! We have some ideas to share about how you can help them skip that stage entirely. Regardless of age, regardless of money attitudes, you need to get your children on the budget program 100 percent. How? Let's get them started with a game.

The Bare Necessities

In her book *10-Minute Life Lessons for Kids*, parenting writer Jamie Miller shares a terrific way to help children open their eyes to what's really important in life. Here's how:

- Gather your family around a blackboard or a large sheet of paper.

- Ask them all to answer the question "Other than air, water, and sun, what are some things it would be hard to live without?"

- Without judging any of their answers, begin
  to write down the suggestions. A typical
  family's list might include things like TV,
  video games, house, bed, computer, electric-
  ity, clothes, toothbrushes, money, love, music,
  family, medicine, movies, air conditioner,
  e-mail, the VCR, furniture, shoes, telephone,
  church, bikes, and so on. Draw up a fairly
  lengthy list before going on to the next step.

- Ask them to take turns crossing an item off
  the list, something they could live without if
  they had to.

Again, without judging, begin to cross off items as
they are suggested. "VCR? You think you can live
without the VCR? Okay, scratch it!" "The computer? Okay, it goes out, too!" There are no right
or wrong answers to this game. After whittling the
list down to just the bare necessities, you might end
up with a list like this: family, love, house, music.
What you're hoping to do is open your children's
(and your own) eyes to the fact that so much of
what we think is absolutely essential for daily life
really isn't, that so much of what we spend our
money on is useless, and that you already have the
bare necessities—each other.

Television Tempters

So much of what children ask for is dictated by
what they see advertised on television. What can
you do about this? One of two things:

- Turn the TV off.
- Teach them about commercials.

In our house, whenever our two boys point excitedly to an ad on television, they hear the following calm response: "That's a commercial, honey. They want you to buy something. We don't buy things we see in commercials." Over and over, Saturday morning after Saturday morning, we try to help them understand that just because they see something on the screen doesn't mean their parents will buy it for them.

Do our boys really understand our point about how "they" want you to buy something? Do they understand that there's a huge advertising industry that exists simply to try to convince people to spend money on things they probably don't need and can't afford? Not yet. We hope as they grow older, they will have a firm grasp of commercialism and consumerism.

But I've Gotta Have It!

How easy for the parents of two young boys to sound smug about standing up to the demands of small children. What about looking a 13-year-old in the eye and denying her request (or demand) for a new pair of extremely expensive sneakers? Let's see how one well-known budget-minded parent handles that sticky wicket.

Amy Dacyezyn, the founder of the *Tightwad Gazette*, gained international fame for her frugal-living newsletter and the books it has spawned. She no longer publishes the newsletter, but her advice on all things frugal is more than valid. Here's what she has to say about teens and consumption:

- Teenagers who want to spend any way they want should earn their *own* money.

- A teen spending his own hard-earned money has a better chance of deciding to forgo expensive and fancy stuff than if he's just out spending his folks' cash without stopping to think about where it came from.

She believes that if the parents are consistent and the rules about spending money are clear, children will do quite happily in a budget-minded family. Our own approach with our oldest son, 10-year-old Julian, has been that he has to earn half of whatever big purchase he craves. That iPod he has? He paid half of not only the iPod, but that expensive warranty, too! We also insist that for every new thing the boys can't live without, they have to get rid of something they already have. They can donate it to charity, and we also let them sell their own stuff on eBay. Julian paid for quite a bit of his iPod by selling a much loved Lego Imperial Star Destroyer.

Such a Nice Grandmother ...

When laying down the new house budget rules, you need to keep a few other folks informed: the grandparents. Of course grandparents love their grandkids and want to indulge them with treats when they can, but if you're trying to wean your kids off the expensive stuff habit, don't let your folks undermine your efforts. "Mom says I can't have XYZ. Will you please buy it for me, Grandma?" And all your efforts go down the drain. So you need to make sure Grandma and Grandpa (and Auntie and Uncle and Stepmom and Godparent and so on) understand the new philosophy and help you reinforce the ideas. This may be tough, but keep at it!

The bottom line is that you must teach your children to save, to make trade-offs (a pair of new jeans instead of a Saturday afternoon at the movies—not both!), and to set limits when it comes to expectations as well as actual dollar limits. What is the absolute best way to teach this? By living it yourself! Teaching your kids by example about the value of money is far better than endlessly lecturing them on the topic.

Cash and the College Kid

After negotiating the rocky budgeting shoals of being newlyweds, and of raising children with a solid sense of the value of money, can you then relax and breathe easy? Sorry, now you have to watch those kids go off to college, and you have to take those phone calls late at night that start off, "Uh, Dad? I've got a little problem here …."

Even the most carefully constructed family budget can be rocked by college kids. Here are just some of the things that could happen:

- Tuition costs much larger than anticipated and planned for

- A burst of immature and irresponsible spending once the student arrives at college, caused by peer pressure and newfound freedom
- Credit-card or checking-account mishandling
- Living costs much higher than anticipated
- Travel costs to and from college
- Increased long-distance bills

Goodness, sounds like we really expect kids to blow it once they go away to college! Of course we don't, but we do want to point out that things like this have happened before (and will happen again). One way to instill good money-management techniques is to teach your children to handle their own money long before they go away. Don't put their suitcase in the dorm room and open their first checking account all in the same day. Better to start small a few years before so that your child grows accustomed to balancing checkbooks and handling money.

As if senior year in high school isn't scary enough for parents to handle, it's also the time that credit-card offers start to appear in the mail addressed to your child. Yikes! What to do? Your first impulse will be to gather them up and stick 'em in the trash before your child gets to the mail. Is that the right way to handle it? Probably not. Sooner or later a piece of mail is going to get through.

If your children have watched you handle credit responsibly for years—paying off the balance every month and not going overboard on impulse purchases—then perhaps they, too, will have good credit-card habits.

But if you haven't always been a stellar citizen in the world of credit, why not share your story with them? It will probably be embarrassing, but try to remember that you're helping your children avoid similar mistakes. Sit them down and tell them the ugly truth about debt.

A Collection Agency on the Line?

And if they blow it? How should you handle it if your son or daughter comes home from his or her freshman year at college with a big stack of credit-card bills and a forlorn expression? Should you bail them out?

The short answer is no. Help them work up a plan to pay their bills off (just as you had to do). Help them develop a budget that lets them avoid creating a similar situation (just as you had to do). But don't write a check and bail them out without any hard work or newly reformed habits on their part, because next year they will show up with an even bigger stack of bills!

Good-Student Bonus

What if your child goes off to college and does a great job handling the money? No calls for extra cash, no stack of unpaid credit-card bills, not even a collect call? Let them know how proud you are. Why not give them a bonus? Just like in the real world where folks get bonuses for a job well done!

Savvy Saver

Not sure what to give your graduating senior as a gift? Never mind the watches and the trip to Disneyland. Buy 'em a book about how to handle money! Peter Lynch's book for beginning investors is *Learn to Earn: A Beginner's Guide to the Basics of Investing and Business.*

Another Very Nice Grandma

At the tiny women's college that Jennifer attended was one student who was known to all for one reason—she got a lavish monthly allowance from her wealthy grandmother, so much money that Jennifer remembers lying awake one night in her dorm room thinking, "How could you possibly spend that much in one month?"

Savvy Saver

Encourage your children to start their own bank accounts in high school, before they go away to college. That way they can build up a little stash of money (not so much that they fail to qualify for financial aid) and get used to handling their own cash.

And how did it all turn out? As an adult, Jennifer's friend has led a rocky financial life. Perhaps she's still hoping someone will send her a big check every month. And Jennifer still lies awake at night wondering how anyone could squander that money!

Another Fifty-Fifty Plan

Remember our plan in Chapter 8 for paying half cash and half credit for big-ticket items? Here's one plan that can help you apply that same theory to college costs.

Bob Dreizler, a Sacramento-based chartered financial consultant and the author of *Tending Your Money Garden*, shared his philosophy with us. "Long before my daughter Sonya went away to school, we sat down together and worked out a contract. I told her, 'Okay, I am giving you X dollars for your college education. In addition, I will loan you X dollars for your college education.' We agreed on a fair interest amount and a repayment schedule that begins after graduation. It was a fairly emotional session, I'll admit."

Why did Bob create this plan? Because as a financial planner, he has seen client after client express real resentment over the fact that their own retirement plans have been jeopardized because they picked up the total tab for their children's college education.

Special Budget Scenarios, Not Sabotage

Weddings, honeymoons, new households, small children, teenagers, and college students—they don't have to wreck your budget. With the advance planning advice you've picked up here, we hope you can see how to best include these situations in your new life on a budget without throwing your hands up in the air in frustration.

The key to any and all special situations? The same key to successful budgeting—planning. Use wisdom and discipline, and teach your family members to use the same wisdom and discipline in their financial dealings. It can be done!

The Least You Need to Know

- Most couples fight about money, but by starting early and designing a budget that works, newlyweds can escape some of that drama.
- Developing common financial and budgeting goals for your marriage can really strengthen you as a couple.
- Teach small children what's really of value—love and family, not candy and action figures.
- Teenagers who lust after fancy clothes and accessories must earn their own cash to squander.

- The financial education of college students should be planned for long in advance. Their first experience with checks and credit cards should not be postponed until they leave home.

- Reward your children for effective money handling and budget-minded behavior.

Chapter

Great Budgeting Resources

In This Chapter

- Online financial calculators can be helpful and easy to use
- Searching the word "budget" brings up more ads than information
- Pie charts can help you to visualize just where the bulk of your money goes
- Budgeting doesn't require an online connection or a computer

There's much talk nowadays about the vast information source that is the World Wide Web— information on topics from the arcane to the absurd. But moving beyond arcane and absurd, where on the web can you find information about living on a budget? All *over* the place!

One small caveat, however. It does seem logical to just drop into a search engine like Excite or Yahoo! and type in "budget" to see what you get. Alas, the word *budget* gets you quite a few search results, but they will all be for *business budgets*. To search out more sites for your own use, use the words "family budget."

Way-Cool Websites

You can find three basic types of family budgeting information in cyberspace:

- Financial calculators
- Advice and tips on saving money and living on a budget
- Newsgroups and online communities devoted to the frugal life

Let's drop in on a few of them and take a look at what they offer.

USA Today

One of our personal favorites is the website run by *USA Today* newspaper: www.usatoday.com. Not only is it a cheapskate's way to save 50 cents a day by reading the newspaper online instead of dropping two quarters in the box, but it's also a terrific source of financial information.

The "Money" section of the online paper includes a "Personal Wealth" subsection that lets you choose to view information about making money, saving money, or spending money (see the green buttons at the very top of the page). You can browse through a lengthy list of past articles that ran in *USA Today* on topics like the high cost of using credit cards for cash advances.

Here's the coolest part of the "Personal Wealth" site—click on the selection marked "calculators." These calculators are powerful tools, enabling you to fill in the blanks with your financial and personal information to get a basic evaluation of home mortgages, bank loans, credit-card use, the cost of cars, personal loans, insurance, and more. There's even a calculator marked "Saving" that enables you to crunch the numbers on questions such as the following:

- Which is better: cash or payments?
- What will it take to become a millionaire?
- What will it take to save for a college education?
- What's it worth to reduce my spending?

This last choice—"What's it worth to reduce my spending?"—is an absolute must for anyone committed to living on a budget. It lets you enter your own dollar figures to see exactly how much you can save annually by reducing the amount of money you spend going out to dinner, going to movies, buying fancy clothes, or buying another car. And then it adds it all up into a total annual savings and lets you know how that saved money will increase in value over the years—a very convincing argument for cutting back on frivolous stuff.

Frugal Family Network

The motto of the folks at Frugal Family Network is "Living Creatively Within Your Financial Means." Founded by two thrifty women who each feed a family of four on less than $175 a month, their site has a number of helpful links to other frugal living and budget living sites and newsgroups. They also have a section on "quick tips from our subscribers," which lists great ideas for cutting costs on things like dental cleanings (go to a local dental school or community college). Alas, they no longer produce their well-written and informative newsletter, but will happily sell you copies of back issues for two dollars an issue. But this is definitely a site worth visiting, at www.frugalfamilynetwork.com.

Money.com

The folks at *Money* magazine also have a superb site. In addition to enabling you to access past articles on a wide variety of financial topics, it, too, has some pretty cool calculator functions.

Do you daydream of someday moving to a small town to have a less costly, more family-oriented lifestyle? You can find out exactly how much you will save (or spend!) moving from one city to another. Click on your current city, click on your dream city, enter a few financial variables, and voilà! Check it out at www.money.com.

You can also enter your age, income, number of family members, and a few other variables, and then find out what the national spending averages are for folks like yourself. Do you suspect you spend too much of your income on housing and insurance? Find out for sure.

Consumer Reports

Not only can you read newspapers like *USA Today* online for free, but you can also find a pretty broad variety of magazines. And what better online magazine for budget-minded folks than the old favorite, *Consumer Reports*. Now that you are fiercely committed to the idea of wise shopping, this is information you will need. How else can you know that the refrigerator you carefully saved for and then paid for in full with cash will continue to serve your family faithfully for the next 20 years? The address is, of course, www.consumerreports.com.

Frugal Living on About.com

This is another handy frugal living site for budget minded folk, filled with articles on topics like "Eating on the Cheap," "Frugal Fun for Kids," and even "Ten Minutes to a More Frugal You." Like many of the other frugality sites, this one has many built-in links that can take you to other money-saving sites.

And here's one of the best things about the Frugal Living site—free budgeting software! So if you have been struggling to draw up the paper-and-pencil budget that we've outlined, toss your early efforts in a drawer and click onto the free budgeting software this site offers. Such a deal! They also send out several free e-zines on different frugal topics.

The web address for the Frugal Living section is http://frugalliving.about.com.

Goals and Jewels

Jennifer started the Goals and Jewels site years ago as an inspirational money site for women, and still maintains it as a way to inspire women to strive for the top and save on their way there … and give themselves a treat or two once in awhile. The best feature is a beautifully decorated blank goals sheet you can print out (do it in color, it's gorgeous) and hang on your wall so your goals are always near you. Go to www.goalsandjewels.com, and then go to the Diamond Room for the blank goals sheet.

The Dollar Stretcher

The motto of this site is "Living Better … for Less," and you'll find dollar-stretching tips on everything from how to throw an inexpensive wedding shower to how to make your own hand lotion. You can also get advice on do-it-yourself auto and home repair. If you don't see the advice you need, you can e-mail your living-on-a-budget question to the Dollar Stretcher himself for an answer. Visit the Dollar Stretcher at www.stretcher.com. Blogging has reached the frugal set (after all, it is free!), and the blog "My Two Cents" on this site is worth a read.

DoItYourself.com

What can you find at a site called DoItYourself.com? Just about everything! Why pay someone to do something for you when you can do it yourself for free? This site lists information and resources on an enormous variety of handyman-type projects, everything from brick and masonry to pest control. Check it out at www.doityourself.com, and see what you can start doing yourself!

eHow.com

Similar in tone and purpose to the DoItYourself site, www.ehow.com is filled with links and info on how to do things without hiring an expert. Check it out and see what you can fix, or do, or figure out how to manage on your own!

Temple of Thrifty Motoring

Who wouldn't want to visit the Temple of Thrifty Motoring? Peter worships there regularly, believing that keeping an old car running is a great frugal practice. Check out the information here; it can help your car stay on the road that much longer. Dr. Dipstik is focused on helping you lengthen the life of your car. Go to http://home.att.net/~drdipstik/home.htm.

Magazines

Although the printed world is awash in big-dollar magazines like *Architectural Digest* and *The Robb Report*, there is also an emerging class of magazines for the less well-heeled. Recent entries include *Budget Savvy*, *Budget Travel*, and *Budget Living*, and each has an idea or two each month that makes it worth the price of the issue. Jennifer also enjoys *Real Simple* magazine, as well as *Martha Stewart Living*. Martha really isn't about spending tons of dough; there are always ideas on how to re-use old items in clever ways as well as simple instructions on how to make all kinds of things, including gift cards, table decorations, and children's toys.

Helpful Newsletters

More interested in reading words on a printed page than on a flickering screen? Don't despair; there are plenty of actual printed newsletters that can bring you lots of helpful information about living on a budget:

> *Living Cheap News*
> PO Box 8178
> Kansas City, MO 64112
> Subscriptions—$12 a year, sample issue free with self-addressed, stamped envelope.

> *Frugal Times*
> PO Box 5877
> Garden Grove, CA 92645
> Subscriptions—$14 a year, sample issue $1.00.

> *A Penny Saved*
> PO Box 3471
> Omaha, NE 68103-0471
> Subscriptions—$14 a year, sample issue $3.00.

> *The Frugal Budget Booster*
> 61 Paul Street
> South Berwick, ME 03908
> Subscriptions—$15 a year, sample issue $2.00.

Big Ideas, Small Budget
2201 High Road
Tallahassee, FL 32303
Subscriptions—$12 a year, sample issue $1.00.

Cheapskate Monthly
PO Box 2135
Paramount, CA 90723-8135
Subscriptions—$18 a year, sample issue free.

Savvy Discounts Newsletter
PO Box 96
Smyrna, NC 28579
Subscriptions—$9.95 a year, sample issue free.

The Frugal Gazette
PO Box 3395
Newtown, CT 06470-3395
Subscriptions—$15.95 a year, sample issue free
with self-addressed, stamped envelope.

Keep Your Cash
PO Box 2234
Holland, MI 49422-2234
Subscriptions—$12 a year, sample issue free
with self-addressed, stamped envelope.

Software Solutions

Now that you know how much information is out
there in cyberspace, is there anything else you can
do with your computer that will help you with
budgeting? Sure, you can buy software packages
that help you keep your finances shipshape.

Using Quicken

The granddaddy of all financial software is Quicken. We will confess right upfront that we don't use Quicken ourselves, but some of our best friends do! And they all tell us that life without Quicken is unthinkable. Once you get started, you will never go back, they claim. Even Jennifer's own mother swears by it.

What's so great about using Quicken? In a nutshell, it's a bill-paying system. Click on "Bills," see what's due, and click a few more times to pay them automatically! No stamps, no fumbling around to match the bill up with the proper envelope. Just click and pay.

Or, if you prefer, click and print. Print out your checks, that is. Many devotees of Quicken use them to print out all their checks for bill-paying.

Is this magic, or what? Not really. Because before any of that information (about your bills) shows up on your computer screen, you must enter it. To get the maximum use out of Quicken or any other financial software, don't overlook the fact that you must first devote many hours to entering all your bill-paying information.

Sound like a big time commitment? It is. For large recurring monthly bills (mortgage payments, for instance), however, it can streamline the process considerably. You can even schedule future payments and send them online or print out the checks when needed.

A Big Slice of Pie

For those of us committed to living the budgeted life, here's what we think is really great about Quicken—the pie charts. You remember pie charts, those colorful wedges that help you visualize important percentages like, say, how many American farmers raise corn (big slice of pie), how many raise wheat (another big colorful slice), and how many raise organic lettuce (very thin slice).

So wouldn't it be neat to see all your expenses divided up into slices of pie? Big wedge of pie for your household expenses, smaller slice (you hope) for clothing, and really thin slice for stereo equipment. When starting out, you might be taken aback by some of your pie slices, but once you start to live your life on a budget, you can adjust the portions accordingly so that the slice of pie representing your savings account, or the slice of pie for your children's college fund, just gets bigger and bigger!

Fear Not

Intimidated by all the high-tech talk you've just waded through? Ready to throw up your hands and declare that it's all too darn complicated, and you'll never be able to keep up with everything on your computer? Fear not—because if you feel that way, then skip it.

It's still possible to live life in today's society without signing up for all the high-tech bells and whistles. You can manage your budget with a pencil and a sheet of clean paper. You can even manage your budget in your head, if you'd prefer.

Budgeting does not require a computer. Budgeting does not require an account with America Online. Budgeting does not require an e-mail address.

All budgeting really requires is your belief that life will be easier once you get your spending under control. As we've tried to show you through chapter after chapter, we believe that it is. And we hope we've convinced you, too.

The Least You Need to Know

- A great deal of information is available on the web that can help you save money and live on a budget.

- Many financial websites have calculators that help you make more informed decisions about spending money.

- You can read many magazines and newspapers online for free, and find past articles on topics that interest you.

- There are many informative newsletters on the subject of living cheaply.

- Using Quicken to organize your finances can help you understand where the money goes.

- Although there's helpful information online, and useful software available, neither is required to live on a budget. Use your mind, a piece of blank paper, and a pencil.

Living Happily Ever After

In This Chapter

- How real people really budget
- Reviewing the best reasons to live on a budget
- Money-wise versus frugal living
- The best part—choosing your rewards!

All right! Not long ago, the idea of living on a budget was the furthest thing from your mind—now you've read 10 whole chapters about exactly how to do it! Who'd a thunk it?

But you are determined—determined to bring your financial life under control so that you can live a calmer life, a life in which you no longer have to fear running short at the end of every month, a life in which you can begin to plan how you can acquire some of the things you've longed for, and a life in which you realize that some of what you long for might not be so necessary after all.

Let's eavesdrop on a few real people who believe that living on a budget has made a big difference in their lives.

Real Budgets, Real Voices

- Katy in Granite Bay, California, and her husband, Bob, are both self-employed. "I devised a budget spreadsheet out of a simple 'need to know.' We needed to know exactly how much money we each had to bring in each month to pay our bills! With the budget in place, there is no longer a constant worry in the household. Twice a year, I pull up all the different categories—everything from car insurance to dry cleaning—and take a look to see if I can re-bid or scale back our expenses in that category." Katy plans to move her entire budget from the spreadsheet she designed to the Quicken program.

- "We couldn't manage without a budget!" says Kathleen in Grants Pass, Oregon. She and her husband, Richard, own their own small business, which produces most of its income in the spring and summer months. "With seasonal income swings, we need to stay on top of our money. I have a typed budget that includes all the big-expense items. As for little expenses, we try to skip as many of those as we can." Instead of trips to Toys 'R' Us with their two daughters, Kathleen and Richard take them on camping and biking trips. "We spend time with our children instead of lots of money."

- Michelle in Lafayette, Colorado, made the decision to quit her job and stay home with her children almost 15 years ago. Going from two incomes down to one required many changes, but because of their family budget, "We don't feel like we suffer or have anything less than we did before in our lives." As she points out, "You aren't going to be happy if you deny yourself everything!"

This far into the book you may be tired of hearing about the lives of your authors, Peter and Jennifer, but we'll add one last real budget/real voice on this topic:

In almost a dozen years of marriage, we have tried very hard to stay within our budget goals. We are far from saintly when it comes to sticking with the plan, but have managed over the years to carefully (and sometimes casually) adhere to the budget guidelines we decided on years ago. At any given time, we are conscious of where our money is going— whether it's last week's grocery bill, the looming owner's association dues, or the amount added to reserve savings to pay year-end property taxes.

When we wrote the first edition of this book in 1999 our lives were vastly different. Jennifer was a self-employed writer and book packager, and Peter was a corporate employee of a major company with a solid salary and full benefits. But our lives, like so many other Americans, have changed in the past few years. Peter was laid off from that cushy job and has joined Jennifer in the self-employed world. Two uncertain incomes can be scary. Because we already had this living-on-a-budget thing down, we made the transition fairly well. How much money we spend, and when, is even more important to us now.

What's it gotten us? Does this mean we are humorless nickel-and-dimers? Heavens, no! It'll come as a real surprise to our neighbors when they see we've written this book—we look, talk, and act like everyone else in the neighborhood. We also still have one big indulgence—travel. We take nice trips a few times a year, although less often than when our incomes were more secure. How can we afford it? Planning and discipline in other parts of our budget lets us sock away money so we can travel and pay cash for it when we do. When we spend, we spend well, with few regrets. For us, the very real benefits of living on a budget have been the infrequent arguments about money and peace of mind from being prepared for unexpected financial surprises (like Peter's lay-off).

Reviewing the Reasons

To get you pumped up about what a big difference living on a budget is going to have in *your* life, let's go back and review some of the best reasons to adopt it as a way of life:

- You will gain control of your monthly bills.
- You will be prepared and avoid surprises.

- You can finally save for that major purchase—a house, a business, an education.
- You can opt out of the spend-now-pay-later cycle.
- You may be able to expand your lifestyle or retire early.

The *real* benefits aren't even financial:

- Eliminate money as a source of tension. Reduce stress in your life and in your relationships.
- Rediscover that the best things in life are *free!*
- Rest easier knowing that you have escaped the cycle of getting deeper and deeper in debt.

Sounds like so much fun! Shall we tell you again about some of the simple ways to achieve this?

Reviewing the Secrets

Before you even begin to draw up your budget, begin shifting your attitude toward spending money. Start with some of these principles:

- Develop a greater awareness of how you spend money.
- Develop a greater awareness of how others (advertisers, retailers, manufacturers) *want* you to spend money.

- Try to stay out of the "envy trap," and avoid lusting after things that other folks have.

- Delay your purchases. If you wait long enough, you might discover ways to do without buying it!

- Develop solid financial and budget goals for yourself and your family that you can all work toward achieving.

- Set specific personal and family spending limits and *stick to them.*

And *don't* do these:

- Make ends meet with credit cards.

- Abuse cash, cash advances, and ATM machines.

- Cheat (on your budget, that is).

Avoid blunders, and you will be far down the road to success!

Stepping Out with the 12 Steps

We outlined 12 steps that will lead you to a workable budget. Here's a quick review (you will not be tested!):

- Understand your income. Know where it comes from and how it varies throughout the year.

- Understand your expenses. "Financial forensics" give you a picture of all your monthly and irregular expenses.

- Set goals—a few good, realistic goals agreed to among your family.

- Know your habits—how you spend, what tempts you, and where you and your family are exposed to going wrong.

- Set up savings and spending mechanisms that *work*, such as reserve accounts and growth accounts, and having the right number of credit cards.

- Make an income plan. *Detail is important.*

- Plan your obligations, or must-pays. Smooth out large lump-sum bills with reserve accounts. *Detail is important.*

- Plan your necessities, and look for ways to economize. *Detail is important.*

- Set aside pocket money for daily incidentals. *Don't sweat the details.*

- Create a family allowance to cover family entertainment and so forth. *Don't sweat the details.*

- Create a personal allowance for whatever. *Don't sweat the details.*

- Go through it until it balances. Make wise decisions and trade-offs. Get agreement, and then be prepared to stick to it.

Done! You're ready to live happily ever after on a budget.

Taking It to Another Level

Way back in the beginning of this book, we assured you that living on a budget would not be about "frugal living," but rather how to budget for the basic American lifestyle. That's been the mission for all of the chapters you've read so far.

But have we been giving conflicting messages? Sometimes we talk about how to save to buy a boat, and other times we urge considering whether you need a boat at all! Where do we really stand on all this frugal-living/simple-lifestyle stuff? Are we fer it or agin' it?

Although Jennifer harbors dreams of someday living in a hillside home off the grid, we live in a Northern California suburban neighborhood surrounded by big-box stores. Not exactly living the simple back-to-nature life.

We really don't live what is often described as a "frugal life." We live on a budget, but we don't re-use vacuum cleaner bags, make our own granola, or leave the air-conditioning off in the summer. Shoot, we'll even confess to owning three cars on occasion (make no mistake—the newest one is a five-year-old former company car purchased used, with 13,000 miles, at two thirds the new price).

However, we have consciously chosen to bypass some of the other basic trappings of American life—no cable TV, no fancy clothing, no idle trips to the mall. Jennifer buys a fair portion of her clothing from upscale resale shops, and Peter always buys on sale, out of season. Our children are enthusiastic garage-sale shoppers, always on the lookout for toys and video games they can buy for a quarter or two.

Savvy Saver

You needn't feel alone as you try to change your lifestyle. There's an active online community of folks who believe in living on less. In a lengthy newsletter about living on a budget, one couple shared the following philosophy: "To us, it is not worth having to work the rest of our lives so that we can have the latest toys and the largest house and the fancy SUV *now*."

Frugal Living

Still, there's a growing frugal-living movement sweeping the country. Once you're really living on a budget, you might just decide that goals could be accomplished even faster by scaling down expenses even further. Where do you find more about redesigning your life into frugal-living mode?

Alternatives for Simple Living is a good website to check out (http://members.aol.com/AltSimLiv/simple.html). This site will lead you into an active online community devoted to helping other folks learn more about how to cut way, way, way back on living expenses. You'll find everything from how to save money on weddings to information on constructing a solar oven (sounds wacky, but we know someone who has one and it's pretty cool).

Your Money or Your Life: Your Choice

If you go deeper into frugal living, you might also want to check out the book that has inspired so many people to re-examine why they work and how they live: *Your Money or Your Life*.

Joe Dominguez and Vicky Morgan, the authors of *Your Money or Your Life*, advocate a two-pronged plan:

- Cut your expenses to the bone.
- Put every dime you can into buying Treasury Bills.

When the income you earn from your T-Bills can cover your teeny, tiny living expenses, *quit your job and do whatever you want!*

It really is a fascinating book that opens your eyes to just how readily we toss our hard-earned money away. Even if you don't want to follow their program (and there are other investments than T-bills), we recommend reading the book to gain a different perspective. What perspective is that? Simple—the more you consume, the more you have to work to pay for it. Consume less, and work less to pay for it all. Makes sense, doesn't it?

Reward Yourself, Reward Your Family

Uh-oh. Gosh, we're *almost done* with this manu-script, and we left something out! There's a step 13! Now, don't run down to the bookstore just yet for a refund. We'll take care of it right now.

Step 13, for you triskaidekaphobes, is the best one of all. You made it! Crossed the budget finish line, and have money left over at the end of the month. Crowds, including your family, are cheering. It's time to celebrate!

Any budget plan successfully developed and carried out deserves recognition and reward, in our opin-ion. It is truly an achievement, and, for most of us, it involves sacrifices. So why not indulge a little? If you're successful, the bills are paid, the savings are tended to—go for it!

Every year, we reward ourselves with a Christmas gift-giving season that might seem lavish to some. We also share some of it, sitting down on Christmas Eve to write five to ten checks to our favorite char-ities. The tax benefits pale by comparison to the emotional satisfaction. It's not just "doing good"; it's also a reward for patience and persistence dur-ing the rest of the year.

The Final Budget Message

You've read enough on the topic of budgets. Before we move on to the final chapter on saving at the cash register, we will leave you with the three main principles that, put into practice, will lead you in the right direction:

- Wisdom—best choices and decisions
- Discipline—stick to them
- Honesty—no cheating

The Least You Need to Know

- Living on a budget can help self-employed people and business owners smooth out their financial lives.
- Living on a budget enables many families to live on one, instead of two, incomes, enabling one parent to stay home with the children.
- Don't ever make ends meet with a credit card, abuse cash advances, or go overboard with ATM withdrawals.
- Beyond budgeting, there is frugal living, the idea that if you cut way back on your consumption, you will not have to earn as much to support your lifestyle.
- You must reward yourself in some way for a job well done (living on a budget); otherwise, it will seem like a constant chore.

Chapter  12

Great Ways to Save Money on Just About Anything

In This Chapter

- Great websites that will make a difference in your budget
- How "freecycling" can get you what you need for free
- Taking a part-time job can help you buy for less
- Buying off-season to save

Over and over we've mentioned how much easier life can be if you decide not to fill your life up with costly items. But hey, sometimes you've just got to bust lose and spend some money! Hard as we try to ignore the "spend, spend, spend" messages around us, we aren't always immune either. And when that impulse hits we sit down and try to figure out how to get what we want for less. Much less. Free if possible!

Figuring out how to save money can be a real intellectual exercise, one that uses all of your imagination, skill, and memory. Sometimes charm helps, too. A recent trip that Jennifer took to Legoland is an example: she remembered that she had flight coupons that were expiring, so she called around until she found out how to get the best discount on the admission price (it was with our AAA auto club membership), and she negotiated with a hotel she'd stayed at just a few short weeks before and managed to get them to come down from the tourist rate to the corporate rate she'd paid before. After putting together all of these elements she saved hundreds of dollars on a two-day trip with our six-year-old. She also felt a real sense of triumph at using all of her skills to achieve the savings.

Here are our favorite ways to save money on just about anything, from necessities like dental work to frivolities like perfume and jewels.

Savvy Saver

Frugality leads to using your imagination, to stretching your brain (and sometimes your body) in new and challenging ways. It gives you a new way to look at what you already have in your life and ask yourself the question … Hmmm … what else can I use this for? What else can I do with this? Or better yet, how can I do *without* that?

Save Money on Real Estate Transactions

Sell a house, and lose a hefty chunk of the price to a realtor. Realtors are very nice people, but can you do without them and keep that money in your pocket? Yes, you can sell your house on your own; Peter has successfully sold two houses on his own and is a fan of the do-it-yourself method. You can market it on your own locally with signs, flyers, and word of mouth, but you can also use custom services like www.forsalebyowner.com or www.owners.com who help in the process and get your house into the Multiple Listing Service in your area. Do spend the money on a good real estate attorney or escrow officer though, to make sure you aren't leaving yourself legally vulnerable in any way.

The same savings can work for buying a house, too. If you are willing to work with a DIY seller, at least some of the savings should flow your way. Understand that they are saving a chunk on transaction costs and try to strike a deal accordingly.

Save Money on Arts and Entertainment

Movies, plays, and concerts really can be free, if you pay close enough attention. Many newspapers give away free tickets to brand new movies with promotions (watch your local newspaper). Love the theater but can't afford the ticket price? Why not ask if you can be a volunteer usher? There is a whole group of folks who are volunteer ushers in New York's Broadway theater district. Ask one of the folks who shows you to your seat next time how to get started. Ask in your own hometown, too, of course; your local theater could certainly use the help.

We find that belonging to the local art museum (here in our town it is the oldest museum in the West—The Crocker Art Museum) gives us access to all manner of free events. Jazz concerts in the courtyard, puppet performances for kids, and dance recitals on the weekends—the invitations never stop coming and our annual membership fee is earned back many times. On trips to New York we've gone to the Guggenheim for their free jazz concerts on Friday evenings. Check out the museums in your area; you'll be surprised at what they offer. Most major museums also offer a day or evening at least once a month when the admission price is either reduced or outright free.

Becoming a member of the local NPR station also gives us access to free events, and at the same time we are supporting something we believe in.

Save Money on Electronics

Overstock.com is a good source to check for well-priced consumer electronics. Peter also recommends going to manufacturer websites to check if they sell refurbished equipment directly to consumers themselves.

When talking to electronics salespeople, always ask if they have any refurbished or "open box returns" that could be had for less. Our first DVD player was purchased that way and has never disappointed us.

Save Money in the Garden

A thriving garden is a delight, and you can avoid the cost of buying flowers elsewhere! But seeds and plants can add up, too. Jennifer stays away from overspending in nurseries by asking other gardening friends for cuttings of plants and starting them in water before transplanting outside.

By creating your own compost you will not only help cut down on garbage but also create dense rich soil in which your own plants can thrive. You can easily make your own compost frame; check out the plans on www.gardenplace.com.

Here are a few other tips:

- Starbucks gives away used coffee grounds to gardeners who request it. You might have to bring your own plastic bag to transport the grounds, but it's worth it! Coffee grounds start life fairly acidic, but by the time they are brewed the ph factor ends up around 6.9 and it can be a nice nutrient for your soil. Ask at your local Starbucks.

- The www.stealitback.com website, which features stuff from police evidence rooms, offers growlights for sale on a regular basis. (Gee, I wonder what the bad guys were using those for?)

One of the biggest gardening purchases is a lawn-mower. Peter is proud of the refurbished Craftsman lawnmower he bought from Sears, for a cost savings of 40–50 percent. Always ask the salespeople on the floor if there are any refurbished or returned models available for less.

Save Money on Travel

Despite our frugal ways in most areas, we do like to travel, and we do like to stay in swanky hotels. How can we do that and still stay on a budget? Research, luck, and the willingness to travel when other folks aren't. Because, hey, even the Ritz-Carlton goes on sale sometimes. Diana Gil-Osorio of the Ritz-Carlton at Half Moon Bay suggests asking when the low season is and making your travel plans accordingly. At the Half Moon Bay location (on the California coast south of San Francisco), for instance, the low rates are available from mid-November through mid-March.

We've also found that belonging to the "frequent stayers" programs at many hotels can really pay off in savings. By belonging to the Starwood Preferred program we were able to get a bargain rate at a fancy Sheraton on Kauai, and saved money on the daily resort fee as well. We've also received invitations to visit new hotel properties for stunningly low rates, $175 a night instead of $595 a night. Hard to pass up those kinds of deals!

We have a few favorite budget travel sites that we cruise all the time. Yahoo's Fare Chaser can do your work for you in hunting down the lowest airfare. You can find them at www.farechase.yahoo.com and it will search dozens of sites for the cheapest air, hotel, or rental-car prices.

Remember, the more flexible you are about where you're going and when you really need to be there, the better you can scoop up the bargains. We make it a point to be relaxed enough about our schedules that if the flight is asking for volunteers to give up their seats and take a later flight, and offering travel vouchers and incentives, we volunteer! This doesn't work with business travel, of course, but if you can do it once or twice a year you might end up with another trip for free.

Here are some other travel tips:

- Our favorite bargain travel site is Suntrips (www.suntrips.com), where it's possible to get last-minute deals on charter trips to Hawaii, Mexico, Costa Rica, and the Caribbean. Sometimes we buy the whole package from them—hotel, air, and a rental car, or sometimes just the airfare to Hawaii and then we find cheaper hotel prices on our own.

- A cheap source of rooms for travelers to Europe can be found at colleges and universities; check out Reidsguides.com for more information. In London you can stay at Kings College for less than thirty pounds! Call 44-0-20-78481700 to book. And for bargain hunters on their way to Paris, staying at a hospital might be the way to go.

The Hotel-Dieu Hospital has a special floor devoted to hotel guests. For information call 33-1-44-32-01-00.

- One of our best investments has been our membership in the AAA auto club. Not only do we have peace of mind when it comes to being stranded by the side of the road (and Jennifer has gotten her money out of that function!), but we find it to be a tremendous discount generator. Whenever we stop at a hotel we always ask—Do you have a AAA member discount? Sometimes it's just a few dollars, but sometimes it's a hefty percentage. We also get discounts on all manner of other purchases, from the admission price to theme parks to some auto repair services like lubricating to seemingly unrelated purchases like Amtrak tickets. It is worth many times the amount we pay for it every year.

- We don't live in an area that is much sought after by foreign tourists, but those of you who do should try house swapping. You swap your primary or vacation home with someone in another destination. Check it out on digsville.com and see if it might work for you.

Save Money on Food

Our favorite date is, as you might imagine, a frugal one. We go to a local steak house that also serves food in their bar and sit together at a small bar table and split one large serving of prime rib. We each get our own glass of bourbon, of course—you can't skimp everywhere! Sitting so close and sharing one plate feels like the grown-up version of a malt-shop date and we save money and calories, too. Try it.

For the times when we actually want to have dinner in a restaurant, Jennifer keeps a close eye on the two-for-one coupons in the local newspapers. She also keeps up on what restaurants are available through Restaurant.com (www.restaurant.com). There are over 6,000 participating places, so check the site and see who belongs in your area—it's a great deal. You can buy a $25 gift certificate for only $10. That is a major savings on the price of a meal.

Here are some other tips:

- Don't forget the annual "Free cone day" that Ben & Jerry's holds nationwide every year. In 2005 it was April 19th. Ask your local Ben & Jerry's when it is coming up this year!

- The Grocery Outlet chain is another favorite of our family. We don't go there for our regular shopping (although Peter does do most of the shopping at Food Source, a low-priced chain in the West) but stop in on occasion to see what kinds of great deals there are. Wine finds are sometimes worth the trip.

- A great way to keep food costs down is to produce it yourself. In our neighborhood we turned a large patch of unused yard into a communal vegetable garden shared by four families. It is a wonderful way to spend time with friends (weeding) and a delicious way to keep fresh food on the table throughout the summer. The neighbors also share a compost bin, producing our own fertilizer and keeping our garbage use down.

Save Money on Clothing

Jennifer is a shopper supreme. She hasn't paid full price for her clothing in almost 20 years, preferring instead to make a hunt out of the experience to see what kind of wonderful bargain is out there to be found. Sometimes they are online—vintage designer clothing on eBay—and sometimes she finds them at the local designer consignment stores in our area. When we travel anywhere in the country Jennifer reaches for the yellow pages and checks under "consignment." She has found amazing deals on used designer brands in Detroit, Chicago, Cincinnati, Carmel, and Newport Beach. She is most proud of her three-dollar Levi's, purchased at a thrift store in California's wine country. Don't be held back by the idea that someone else once owned these things, just enjoy the fact that you can own expensive clothing for a fraction of the original price.

For those who prefer buying clothing that no one else has owned before, you can always find a sale on somewhere. Make it a game in your life to never pay full price. Check up on the frequent sales that department stores have at the end of the season and plan your purchases accordingly.

Here are a few online sources:

- **www.swapstyle.com.** A free online swap party where you can exchange what you own for what someone else owns. Check it out. The first year of membership is free, and it costs $19.95 after that.

- **www.bagborroworsteal.com.** Why didn't someone think of this earlier? For high-priced handbag addicts, here is a way to belong to a lending library of purses. You pay a monthly membership from 19.95 to as much as 149.95 (depends on the price range of the bags you want to borrow) and you can borrow away. Just like having a rich friend who lets you rummage through her closet.

- **www.citymoda.com.** If you just have to own that purse, check out this site for big savings on designer handbags like Fendi, Prada, and others.

- **www.overstock.com.** The big O has good deals on clothing on occasion, like designer jeans.

- **www.offtherunway.com.** Designer clothing at 60–80 percent off retail price, but the selection is very limited.

- **www.unclaimedbaggage.com.** Here is where unclaimed baggage and its contents ends up. Some is good, some isn't. See what you can find (and maybe some of it is yours if you've ever lost your suitcase!).

123 By the Numbers

Jennifer is fond of the magazine *Real Simple*. Filled with ideas on how to live more simply, it also has great articles on things like 10 ways to use a cheap bottle of vinegar for household cleaning tasks. And it isn't filled with glossy ads for expensive items that create new and costly desires in the readers!

Save Money on Golf

Golf really doesn't have to be a rich man's sport. Doesn't have to be a rich woman's sport, for that matter, or the exclusive terrain of rich kids. All manner of classes and tournaments are organized by your city parks and recreation department at a fraction of the cost of a country club membership, but there are also ways to golf for less at major courses around the country. These websites list information on last-minute online golf discounts:

- www.lastsecondteetimes.com has info for courses in Maryland and Virginia.

- www.standbygolf.com and www. ownthezonegolf.com/discount_tee_times. htm has information for Arizona, California, Florida, Hawaii, Nevada, Oregon, and Texas.

Peter and his golfing buddies keep careful track of the twilight times and prices on their favorite course and know exactly when to arrive in order to spend the least amount possible.

Save Money on Cookware and Small Appliances

Jennifer is devoted to the Tuesday Morning group of stores and hasn't bought a pot or pan anywhere else for years. All of the super fancy cookware we received years ago as wedding gifts has been joined on the shelf by the same high-end brands, but this time she bought them at Tuesday Morning for a fraction of the department store price. Need a crock-pot? Check there first. A new coffee maker? Bought it for $20 instead of $40. It's all in the thrill of the hunt, and the stock changes regularly. If there is something you really want, you might have to check back a few times over a few months before you can find one. But don't give up. You can also check out their website at www.tuesdaymorning.com if they don't have a store near you.

- www.overstock.com also carries a fair selection of small appliances and cookware.
- www.crateandbarrel.com has good prices on last season's merchandise.

Save Money on Furniture

All those model home communities that have sprung up everywhere have created a great opportunity for bargain shoppers. The furniture that is used to make the model look attractive will sooner or later show up for sale somewhere else at a fraction of the price. Check in your area or ask a homebuilder where they sell their used furniture. Here in the Sacramento area there is a store called Encore that specializes in this type of merchandise, and they have a huge warehouse stuffed with high-end furniture and decorator accessories. Wherever there are model homes, there is someone selling that furniture, trust us.

Freecycling

First there was recycling, and now, *freecycling*. Freecyclers are folks who want to give their unused stuff to other people for free. Check out freecycle.org to join the list in your area, and you can post what it is you need—a couch, for instance, or a washer/dryer—and you might be able to find someone who will give you their old one.

 Moneywise Meanings

Freecycle—Giving away your unwanted possessions directly to another person instead of donating them to an organization.

Also check out Craigslist.org. Craigslist got its start in the San Francisco Bay Area and now has sites for many cities. Check out the freebies section on Craigslist to find all kinds of free furniture.

Do It Yourself

Garage sales are still a prime source of inexpensive furniture, and you might find something really amazing. One of the best techniques is to find an old piece of furniture with "good bones" and then reupholster it to fit into your home and design scheme. Upholstery isn't cheap, but it might be less than buying a new couch if you've paid so little to begin with.

You could also take an upholstery class and do it yourself! Jennifer thinks the upholstery class she took through an adult learning center in our area is the best $100 she has spent in a long time. With these new skills, she has redone dining chairs, ottomans, and footstools, saving hundreds of dollars in the process.

There are bargain furniture sites online like homegoods.com, but we aren't sure the savings are really there. The prices look pretty good, but don't overlook how much it will cost to ship. And if it turns out to be a piece of furniture you hate, imagine how much it will cost to ship it back! You're better off looking for furniture bargains in your own regional backyard, where you can toss it into the back of a pickup truck and haul it home for free.

Save Money on Cars

We've talked about cars before, probably more than once. As Americans, the amount of our income that is spent on automobiles is shocking. Money that could be put to use elsewhere, we believe.

Peter is a firm believer in buying a car, and keeping it running for years. And years. And even more years. Learn to do as much as you can to keep it running to keep the costs even lower. The websites we mentioned in Chapter 10 like doityourself.com and eHow.com are filled with information on how to do basic car upkeep and repairs.

Sometimes your needs exceed the car you already own, and that can often lead to the impulsive purchase of a new car. All of a sudden you have out-of-town visitors and they won't all fit into the sedan you own. A van suddenly seems important. Or the couch you bought at a garage sale (heeding our advice in the earlier entry) won't fit in the back of your small pickup and suddenly you feel the need for one of those really huge ones. Okay, take a deep breath. Instead of buying more car than you need, you will save money by owning a basic car for year-round use, and renting once or twice a year to accomplish those special tasks.

When it comes to buying cars, we do believe in buying a slightly used car. We've had good luck with used fleet cars, and are impressed with the CarMax national chain. CarMax has late-model cars that can be bought in a no-nonsense deal at thousands off the price of a new one, with a small warranty included.

Save Money on Building and Remodeling

You know what we're going to say, don't you? *Do it yourself.* It can seem so impossible, we know, but you really can learn these skills. Why not volunteer with an organization like Habitat for Humanity in order to hone your building skills before trying to put them to use around your house? There is also an organization called rebuildingtogether.com that could use your help while you use them to learn. Your local Home Depot has classes every weekend that can help you learn or refine skills to help you keep the costs down when remodeling.

Budget Bombs

Peter likes to warn against "false economies," things that appear to be a good deal that really aren't. One of his prime targets is the idea that frugal folks should shop around for the best gas price. A false economy. Like other utilities, you really should concentrate more on actual consumption than the price. Drive less, save more.

Craigslist, mentioned above as a source for free furniture, can also be a place to find tradesmen who are willing to trade skills and services for something you might already own or know how to do. Swap a fishing boat for a carpet-laying job? It could happen. Trade your copywriting skills for help with your roof? Maybe. Check out what is available and see what will work!

Save Money on Spas and Beauty Services

You can get a movie-star quality makeup job for absolutely free, almost any time you feel like it. How? By plopping down at the make-up counter in a major department store and letting the saleswoman have her way with you. Of course she really wants you to buy all of the makeup she is applying to you, but if you can resist the urge it's the ultimate luxury bargain.

Other luxury bargains are manicures, pedicures, and facials that are available at your local beauty college for reduced rates. While earning their licenses, aspiring estheticians need to perform hundreds of hours of service and you can benefit as a result. Call your local beauty college to see what is available.

Perfume can also be free. While you are getting your face made up for free at the makeup counter you can spritz your wrists with the various perfume testers. There are also many ways to use the perfume strips that come inside of every magazine, too. Rip them out and leave one in your purse, or in your car, for a nice scent.

Here are two other tips:

- www.missthrift.com is a good site filled with info on special prices, discounts, and deals on all kinds of beauty products.

- For spa deals, www.spafinder.com includes a section on "best buys" that links you to the spa deals available at hotels and resorts. A recent special featured La Costa outside of San Diego, for 30 percent off rack rates.

Save Money on Dental Work

Some dentists and hygienists are willing to give small price breaks and discounts to folks who are available to come in at the last minute to fill-in for cancellations. Ask your dentist if they have that policy and if so, ask to be on the list.

Tooth cleaning for reduced prices might also be available at your local community college or technical school where hygienists are being trained.

Save Money on Jewelry

Have you been to a bead store lately? Stringing beads is no longer a pastime of little girls, and bead stores now stock an amazing array of semiprecious stones and beads. Those funky, chunky turquoise bracelets you see in magazine ads? You can easily make one yourself for a fraction of the department store cost. Bead stores also have classes on a regular basis, and you can learn to make your own chandelier earrings, or even luxury items like beaded lampshades.

If there isn't a good bead store near you, check out www.firemountaingems.com for a big selection of semi-precious stones and freshwater pearls.

123 By the Numbers

Jennifer loves black pearls, but hates the retail price on what she sees advertised. Pretty pricey stuff. So what to do? She embarked on a year-long black pearl adventure, surfing eBay for bargains to bid on and visiting wholesale pearl sites online, buying one pearl at a time, until one day she had enough to make an entire strand! It cost a few hundred dollars to put together a short strand of black pearls that would cost many thousands in a retail store. So make an adventure out of getting what you want for less. It can be exciting!

Save Money by Working

We don't mean saving extra money by adding income, we mean saving money by getting a discount where you work! Last year Peter took a part-time job at a Restoration Hardware store in the local mall, just to get the heck out of the house every so often. Even though he only works 10 or 15 hours a week he is entitled to the employee discount of 40 percent. When it comes to making major purchases like bedroom furniture or redwood lawn chairs, a 40 percent savings is huge. One thrifty woman took a part-time job there and bought a complete living room set her first week on the job!

So what is it that you want? Jewelry? Plastic surgery? Travel? If there is a big goal that you aspire to, perhaps adding an extra part-time job to your life will help you get it for less. Most retail stores routinely give their employees a large discount. And yes, plastic surgeons let their staff have free or reduced procedures. Travel? Agents go all over the place for free; that might be the part-time job for you! Be creative about getting what you want for less, and enjoy the thrill and satisfaction of snagging a bargain.

Save on Catalog Purchases

Next time you get any catalog in the mail that tempts you, go and check the company website to see if there is similar merchandise available for less. Watch for a section called sale, outlet, discount, or bargain. It might be last season's merchandise, but it is well worth the savings!

A Few More Thoughts Before We Go

Remember though, the best way to save money on just about anything is to not buy it in the first place. Of course we want you to have a life you enjoy, not one in which you feel deprived, but you choose to react to the advertising messages all around us. Don't let someone else make your life feel empty.

We hope you've enjoyed our thoughts on how to live on a budget, and why it makes for a much more relaxed and stress-free lifestyle. The whole family can benefit in so many ways. Do you have any tips or hints you'd like us to include in future editions of this book? Send 'em on! You can find us online at ginsander@hotmail.com. We love to hear from readers.

The Least You Need to Know

- There is almost always a way to get what you want for less, legally!

- Finding bargains can seem like a real adventure and make life more interesting than just buying like the common folk do.

- Always let your friends and family know what you're looking for; they might give you one for free!

- Take a part-time job at a store that stocks what you want and use the employee discount to save.

Putting Expense Items into Categories

Obligation *Budget Each Item*	Necessity *Budget Each Item*	Pocket Expense *Budget Whole Category*	Family Allowance *Budget Whole Category*	Personal Allowance *Budget Whole Category*
Loan: mortgage	Food, groceries	Lunch at work	Parties, entertaining	Clothing
Rent	Gas	Snacks, sodas	Weekend outing	Hobbies
Association dues	Yard maintenance	Coffee	Movies, etc.	Personal recreation
Insurance: health	Security	Parking	Concerts	Books
Insurance: auto	Pest control	Tolls	Other entertainment	CDs
Insurance: home	Utilities: gas	Newspapers	Home improvements	Manicures
Insurance: renter's	Utilities: electric	Magazines	Home decorating	Hairstyling
Insurance: life	Utilities: garbage	Batteries	Magazine subscriptions	Alterations/shoe repair
Tuition	Utilities: water	Postage	Newspaper subscription	Personal gift

continues

(continued)

Obligation	Necessity	Pocket Expense	Family Allowance	Personal Allowance
Day care	Utilities: sewer	Shipping expenses	Dining out	Luggage
Loan: car	School lunches		Furniture	Night out with friends
Loan: student	Household supplies		Gardening	Collectibles
Taxes: withholding	Car maintenance		Film, processing	Souvenirs
Property taxes	Monthly parking		Video rental	Cell phone
Professional dues	Housekeeper		Sports/recreation	Pager
	Household repair		Family gifts	Small electronics
	Internet service		Contributions	Computer games
	Dry cleaning		Computer software	
	Cable TV			

Appendix B

Great Books for Budgeteers

Bach, David. *Smart Couples Finish Rich*. New York: Broadway Books, 2002.

Dominguez, Joe, and Vicki Robin. *Your Money or Your Life: Transforming Your Relationship with Money and Achieving Financial Independence*. New York: Simon and Schuster, 1999.

Dreizler, Bob. *Tending Your Money Garden*. Sacramento: Rossonya Books, 2003.

Horowitz, Shel A. *The Penny-Pinching Hedonist: How to Live Like Royalty With a Peasant's Pocketbook*. Springfield, MA: Accurate Writing & More, 1995.

Lynch, Peter, and John Rothchild. *Learn to Earn: A Beginner's Guide to the Basics of Business and Investing*. New York: Simon and Schuster, 1996.

Pollan, Stephen M. *Die Broke*. New York: Harper Perennial, 1997.

Sander, Peter. *The Everything Personal Finance Book*. Avon, MA: Adams Media, 2003.

Schor, Juliet B. *The Overspent American*. New York: Basic Books, 1998.

Stanley, Thomas J. and William D. Danko. *The Millionaire Next Door*. Atlanta: Longstreet Press, 1996.

Index